W9-ASN-195

SPORTS HEROES AND LEGENDS

Jackie Robinson

Read all of the books in this exciting, action-packed biography series!

Hank Aaron	Michael Jordan
Muhammad Ali	Sandy Koufax
Lance Armstrong	Michelle Kwan
Barry Bonds	Mickey Mantle
Roberto Clemente	Shaquille O'Neal
Joe DiMaggio	Jesse Owens
Tim Duncan	Jackie Robinson
Dale Earnhardt Jr.	Alex Rodriguez
Lou Gehrig	Wilma Rudolf
Mia Hamm	Babe Ruth
Tony Hawk	Ichiro Suzuki
Derek Jeter	Tiger Woods

SPORTS HEROES AND LEGENDS

Jackie Robinson

by Paul Mercer

BARNES
& NOBLE

NEW YORK

For Noel Lazarus, the most enthusiastic sport fan I know

© 2003 by Lerner Publications Company

This 2003 edition published by Barnes & Noble, Inc. by arrangement with Lerner Publications Company, a division of Lerner Publishing Group, Minneapolis, MN.

All rights reserved. No part of this publication may be reproduced, stored in a retrieval system, or transmitted, in any form or by any means, electronic, mechanical, photocopying, recording, or otherwise, without prior written permission from the publisher.

Cover photograph: Baseball Hall of Fame Library, Cooperstown, N.Y.

Written by Catherine Nichols

Barnes & Noble, Inc.
122 Fifth Avenue
New York, NY 10011

ISBN: 978-0-7607-3471-1

Printed and bound in the United States

14   13   12   11   10   9   8   7   6   5

Sports Heroes and Legends™ is a trademark of Barnes and Noble, Inc.

The quotes in this book have been drawn from many sources, and are assumed to be accurate as quoted in their previously published forms. Although every effort has been made to verify the quote and sources, the publishers cannot guarantee their perfect accuracy.

All Web sites and URLs in this book are current at the point of publication. However, Web sites may be taken down and URLs may change after publication without notice. The Publisher and the Author are not responsible for the content contained in any specific Web site featured in this book, nor shall they be liable for any loss or damage arising from the information contained in this book.

Contents

Prologue
A Day of Destiny
1

Chapter One
A Hard Beginning
5

Chapter Two
The Pepper Street Gang
13

Chapter Three
Four-Letter Athlete
19

Chapter Four
You're in the Army Now
29

Chapter Five
Kansas City, Here I Come
37

Chapter Six
The Great Experiment Begins
45

Chapter Seven
A Royal Man
51

Chapter Eight
Rookie of the Year
61

Chapter Nine
Champions at Last
73

Chapter Ten
Hall-of-Famer
85

Epilogue
Snapping the Barbed Wire of Prejudice
93

Personal Statistics
98

Batting Statistics
99

Fielding Statistics
100

Bibliography
101

Web Sites
102

Index
103

A Day of Destiny

The skies above Roosevelt Stadium in Jersey City, New Jersey, were clear and bright on April 18, 1946. Inside the ballpark over 25,000 fans crowded the bleachers. The press box was jammed with reporters. Photographers swarmed the sidelines, cameras flashing. It was opening day of the sixty-fourth season of the International League, and the Montreal Royals were facing off against the hometown Jersey City Giants. But that wasn't why the air was electric with excitement. The reason behind the capacity-level crowds was one man and one man only. Jackie Robinson, a twenty-eight-year-old from Pasadena, California, was about to make history by becoming the first African American to play major league baseball in the twentieth century. In the mind of every person in the ballpark was one question: "How will he do?"

At the opening ceremony Robinson's heart swelled with emotion. With a lump in his throat, he listened to the words of the national anthem. His heart pounded; his stomach felt like it was full of "feverish fireflies with claws on their feet." Later, he would recall "the parades, the brass band's playing 'The Star-Spangled Banner,' and the marvelous beauty of this 'day of destiny' for me. Nothing else mattered now."

Robinson had more at stake than opening day jitters. Playing in exhibition games with the Royals, a minor league team, he had quickly learned to never know what to expect. During some games he experienced only a few scattered boos. Other times, towns canceled games or locked their ballparks so that Robinson couldn't play there. Once, in Sanford, Florida, the chief of police arrived and ordered Robinson not only out of the game, but out of the ballpark. Racial prejudice was still a fact of life for African Americans. Robinson understood only too well that some people were just not ready for an African American ballplayer.

What would opening day in Jersey City bring, cheers or jeers? On his first at bat Robinson strode to the plate. His hands were sweaty, and he had trouble gripping the bat. After he hit a grounder, the Giants' shortstop easily threw him out. But his second at bat was a different story. Robinson hit a three-run homer. The ball soared off his bat and landed in the left-field stands. Robinson ran around the bases, beaming. The fans didn't know it yet, but Robinson was only warming up.

In the fifth inning, he bunted for a base hit and went on to steal second base. On the next hit, he made it to third. On third, Robinson teased the pitcher, Phil Otis, pretending to try to steal home only to scramble back to base before Otis could throw him out. Again and again Robinson danced on and off third base, agitating Otis more and more. Otis became so confused at Robinson's antics that he balked. When a pitcher balks, pausing too long between pitches, the base runners are allowed to advance to the next base. As soon as the umpire called the balk, Robinson strolled to home plate. Years later, Robinson recalled, "Now the crowd went wild. Not just the Negroes, but thousands of whites, including many Jersey City fans, screamed, laughed, and stamped their feet."

That afternoon the Royals defeated the Giants by a score of 14–1. Robinson, playing in his first game for major league baseball, had not only made history, he had safely hit in four out of five at bats, scored four runs, driven in three, and stolen two bases. It was an impressive performance. Jackie Robinson was on his way to an outstanding career. Baseball would never be the same.

Chapter One

A Hard Beginning

Early on the evening of January 31, 1919, Jack Roosevelt Robinson was born, the youngest of five children. With another mouth to feed, his parents, Jerry and Mallie Robinson, had to work even harder to provide for their family. Mallie and Jerry worked as sharecroppers on a big plantation in Cairo, Georgia. Being a sharecropper was hard work, and most people considered it only one step up from slavery, and not a very high step at that. In the share-cropping system, a plantation owner would give his tenant a piece of his land to farm. In return, the tenant had to give half his crop to the owner. The Robinsons grew cotton, turnips, corn, peanuts, and sugarcane on their land. They also raised hogs, chickens, and turkeys.

When Jackie was six months old, Jerry Robinson deserted his family. Mr. Sasser, the owner of the plantation, wasn't kind to Mallie after Jerry left. Although she still tended to the livestock and her brothers-in-law offered to help bring in the crops, Mr. Sasser evicted her from his land. Mallie took up work as a housekeeper, but more and more she became dissatisfied with life in Georgia. The laws there discriminated against black people. Blacks and whites could not go to school together, or eat together, or ride in the same part of a bus. There were even separate drinking fountains for blacks and whites.

Jackie Robinson was given the middle name Roosevelt in honor of the twenty-sixth president, Teddy Roosevelt.

One day, Mallie's brother arrived from California for a visit. He talked about how wonderful life was out there. "If you want to get closer to heaven," he said, "visit California." Mallie decided that "closer to heaven" sounded pretty good to her. And so, on May 21, 1920, when Jackie was not quite sixteen months old, Mallie packed up her belongings into straw suitcases, gathered her five children, and went to the railroad station. When she boarded the train with Jackie in her arms, she had three dollars sewn into the hem of her petticoat. It was all the money she had in the world.

Mallie arrived in Pasadena, California, in June. She stared in amazement at the groves of orange trees and realized that her brother had been right—California *was* closer to heaven. She wrote home to relatives that her first view of California was "the most beautiful sight in my life." After a few weeks living in an apartment near the railroad station, Mallie and the children moved into her brother's more spacious house.

THE BLACK SOX SCANDAL

The year Jackie Robinson was born, 1919, was also the year major league baseball underwent its biggest scandal. Eight players from the Chicago White Sox were accused of throwing the World Series against the Cincinnati Reds. There was an investigation, and eight players, including "Shoeless" Joe Jackson, one of baseball's best hitters, were indicted. While the seven other players eventually confessed to their part in the scandal, Jackson always maintained he wasn't involved. He once declared: "I am going to meet the greatest umpire of all—and He knows I'm innocent."

Mallie found work as a housekeeper, and although the pay, eight dollars a week, wasn't much, it was more than she earned in Cairo. There was an added bonus, too—she didn't have to work as many hours. The family, though, was still poor. Many times the children ate only two meals a day, and sometimes those meals were nothing more than bread soaked in sweetened milk.

Mallie was determined that her family would do well in California. Although she had to rise before daylight to go to work and often came home exhausted, she still made time for her family. Years later, Jackie remembered "even as a small boy, having a lot of pride in my mother. I thought she must have some kind of magic to be able to do all the things she did, to work so hard and never complain and to make us all feel happy. We had our family squabbles and spats, but we were a well-knit unit."

By the time Jackie was four, all his brothers and his sister were in school. Mallie worked from sunup to sundown. Since Mallie couldn't afford to pay anyone to watch Jackie, she had no choice but to send him to school with his sister, Willa Mae. The teacher allowed Jackie to stay outside and play in the sandbox while Willa Mae watched her younger brother from the window. On rainy days, Jackie was allowed to come into the classroom. This arrangement continued until Jackie was old enough to start school.

In 1922, two years after moving to California, Mallie had scraped together enough money to buy her family a house of their own. It was where Jackie would spend all his growing-up years. The house at 121 Pepper Strèet was quickly christened "the Castle" by family members. And to a small boy like Jackie, it must have seemed like an actual castle. The house was a large one, with five bedrooms and two baths. Bright flowers bloomed in the garden on the front lawn. All kinds of fruit trees covered the property. Jackie could reach up his hand and pluck an apple, peach, orange, or fig. Mallie grew vegetables, and just as she had done back in Cairo, she raised various animals, including turkeys, chickens, ducks, and rabbits.

An Early Influence

Jackie's grandparents, Washington McGriff and Edna Sims McGriff, were born slaves. After her husband died, Mrs. McGriff came to live with her daughter's family. She made a strong impression on young Jackie. She told him never to forget his value in the world and reminded him that no one had the right to look down on him just because of the color of his skin.

But life at the Castle wasn't always a fairy tale. The house was in a mostly white neighborhood. Except for the Robinsons, every family on the block was white. Most of their neighbors didn't want the Robinsons to move in. They tried to buy Mallie out, and when that didn't work, they signed a petition against the Robinsons. Once someone even burned a cross on the front lawn. Jackie was too young to remember the incident, but his older sister, Willa Mae, recalled that "it was in the first year we were there. It wasn't in the middle of the night, either; it was in the evening when everybody was awake. My oldest brother, Edgar, went outside and put the fire out." But the Robinson family refused to be intimidated. The Castle was their home, and they were staying put.

When Jackie was eight years old, he had his own run-in with prejudice. How he faced that challenge told a lot about the kind of person he would become. One day a girl who lived on

---

66*Ever since I can remember, he always had a ball in his hand.*99

—Willa Mae Robinson,
Jackie Robinson's sister

---

his block picked on him, calling him names. Jackie was angry and called her names right back. The girl's father, overhearing the children, rushed out of his house, enraged. He picked up rocks and began throwing them at Jackie. Jackie didn't think twice. He picked up his own rocks and threw them at the man. The rock throwing continued until the man's wife came out and scolded her husband for fighting with a child. It must have been scary for a young boy of eight to have a fight with a grown man, but Jackie wasn't one to back down. He gave as good as he got.

Mallie encouraged this fighting spirit in her children. While she didn't tolerate them starting trouble, she taught them never to accept second-class treatment. She set an example by refusing to be intimidated by her neighbors. It took many years, but eventually the family was accepted. Most neighbors came to respect Mallie. She, in turn, didn't hold a grudge, and when a local bakery gave her its leftovers, rather than let them go to waste, she shared the food with her neighbors on Pepper Street—even the rock-throwing ones.

Chapter Two

The Pepper Street Gang

By all accounts, Jackie was a mischievous little boy. Sid Heard, a childhood friend, recalled the first time he met Jackie. Heard and a friend were waiting to be picked up after the school day ended. Suddenly Heard felt something hit the back of his neck. He swiveled around and saw Jackie "sitting on the edge of the sandbox, shooting small acorns like marbles at us and smiling."

In school, Jackie was a good but not exceptional student. In elementary school, his grades were mostly Bs and Cs. His teachers liked him, and when he came to school hungry, as he sometimes did, they usually had a sandwich ready to share with him.

Although Jackie didn't always excel in the classroom, he did at sports. Classmates would offer him food and money to play on their teams. It seemed like there wasn't a sport or game he wasn't good at. In games of dodgeball, Jackie was always the last player left. Sometimes it would get so late, the children would have to stop the game before it was over because no one had been able to catch Jackie. Soccer and handball were also favorite sports. Ray Bartlett, a childhood friend, recalled, "At lunchtime, we'd have a little time and get into these games. Was he good? He was good at any game he took up. I think maybe soccer and handball required these moves everybody later saw in baseball, but I don't know. He was just an outstanding athlete from the start." He was so outstanding that he led his third-grade soccer team in a victory over the sixth-grade team.

❝I might have become a full-fledged delinquent.❞
—JACKIE ROBINSON

Jackie also loved to play marbles. He would get up early in the morning and play from eight o'clock to five o'clock. Most of the time he didn't even stop for lunch. By the end of the day he'd walk away, having won most of his friends' marbles. According to one childhood friend, Jackie "cleaned us out. He could concentrate. He could concentrate better than any of us." Whenever Jackie put his mind to something, he didn't stop until he succeeded.

As Jackie grew older, he became friends with a group of boys his age from the neighborhood. They named themselves the Pepper Street Gang. The friends were a hodgepodge of nationalities. Jackie later wrote, "Our gang was made up of blacks, Japanese, and Mexican kids. All of us came from poor families and had extra time on our hands."

Usually the extra time was spent on sports. But sometimes, especially as the boys grew older, the time was spent on mischief. None of the mischief was especially serious, at least not by today's standards. The group would throw clods of dirt at passing cars, take fruit off produce stands, or snatch balls off the golf course and later resell them to golfers. One time, a golfer discovered what Jackie was up to. He challenged Jackie to finish playing the hole with him. If the golfer won, he'd keep his ball. If Jackie won, he'd get the ball plus a dollar. Jackie agreed to the terms at once, even though he had never played golf. To the golfer's surprise, Jackie won and was given his prize. Another time, Jackie and his friends tarred the lawn of a neighbor who had earlier called them names. When Mallie found out about this prank, she made Jackie and his

---

❝It kills me to lose. If I'm a troublemaker . . . then it's because I can't stand losing. That's the way I am about winning—all I ever wanted to do was finish first.**❞**

—JACKIE ROBINSON

---

friends clean every bit of tar off the lawn until the grass was green again.

Jackie, in particular, seemed to have a lot of energy that sometimes got him into trouble. A childhood friend remembered how Jackie always managed to get them thrown out of movie theaters. His friend recalled, "Whenever there was a newsreel of Joe Louis [a famous boxer], Jackie would start up going, *Wham! Bam! Pow!* Stuff like that—man, he would just carry on, you couldn't stop him. And sure enough, they'd come over and ask us to leave."

One hot summer's day, Jackie's high spirits got him into bigger trouble than usual. It was a hot day, and Jackie wanted to cool off with a swim. He talked a bunch of his friends into going down to the local reservoir. The reservoir was off-limits to swimming, but that didn't stop Jackie. He and his friends scaled the fence and went for a refreshing swim. The police, however, were waiting for them when they came out and hauled the entire group off to jail.

Luckily for Jackie, around this time he met two men who offered him guidance and helped him to change his ways. One was Karl Downs, pastor of the Robinson family's church. Downs encouraged Jackie to attend church regularly and to teach Sunday school.

Another was a young garage mechanic named Carl Anderson. Anderson liked young people, and he went out of

MACK ROBINSON, OLYMPIC MEDALIST

One summer day in 1936, the Robinson family woke at two A.M. and huddled around the radio to hear the Olympics being broadcast from Germany. Mack Robinson, Jackie's older brother, was scheduled to compete in the finals of the 200-meter dash. The race was neck and neck between Mack and another black athlete, Jesse Owens. In the end, Owens finished first and Mack came in second, winning a silver medal. All the Robinsons, but especially Jackie, were proud of him.

his way to help them. When the local Boy Scouts refused to admit blacks, Anderson founded the first black troop in Pasadena. Anderson saw the trouble Jackie was getting into, and he counseled him to behave himself. Jackie later wrote about Anderson, "He made me see that if I continued with the gang it would hurt my mother as well as myself. . . . He said it didn't take guts to follow the crowd, that courage and intelligence lay in willing to be different." Jackie took the advice of both men and soon was back on the right track.

During the time he was a member of the Pepper Street Gang, Jackie was also attending John Muir Technical High School. Muir Tech had an outstanding sports program, and before long

Jackie had established himself as a star player, earning awards in baseball, football, basketball, and track. No matter what sport he was playing, Jackie was noted as being an unselfish player. He didn't hog the ball or the limelight. Jackie was proud of his achievements. "I enjoyed having that kind of reputation," he said, "but I was also very much aware of the importance of being a team man, not jeopardizing my team's chances simply to get the spotlight."

As if excelling in four sports wasn't enough, on September 6, 1936, Jackie entered the Pacific Coast Negro Tennis Tournament. Jackie hadn't played tennis all that much, but having entered, like always, he became determined to win. And win he did, capturing the junior boys' singles championship.

By the end of Jackie's senior year, he was recognized as an up-and-coming young athlete. The Pasadena *Star-News* singled him out, saying he was "an outstanding athlete at Muir, starring in football, basketball, track, baseball, and tennis." As graduation day neared, Jackie knew that his future lay in the world of sports.

Chapter Three

Four-Letter Athlete

Without any major universities begging to admit him, Robinson enrolled in Pasadena Junior College, home of the Bulldogs, in 1937. The choice wasn't a bad one. The college had a good reputation, tuition was free, and because there weren't any dormitories, students lived at home and commuted. Out of the 4,000 students who went there, only sixty or seventy were black. On campus Robinson saw many familiar faces, both white and black, from his high school days.

In his first year at Pasadena, Robinson easily made the Bulldogs' baseball team, playing shortstop. He was also the team's leadoff batter. He rarely struck out. Even in college he was an expert at stealing bases and at keeping opposing pitchers on their toes. In one memorable game he managed to steal second, third, *and* home. By the end of the year, thanks to Jackie Robinson, the Bulldogs had enjoyed one of the most successful seasons in the history of the college.

Robinson also dominated on the football field. Nicknamed "Jitterbug Jackie" because of his quick moves, he was an ace scrambler and able to run at great speed. He could then stop suddenly, change direction, and dash off again at top speed, leaving slower opponents tackling air. His first season on the team, he scored 131 points and carried the ball for over 1,000 yards. Needless to say, the Bulldogs won the Junior College Championship.

That first semester Robinson also made his mark in track and field, becoming the college's second-best broad jumper. The first was his brother Mack. And in basketball he was the leading scorer on his team. In all, Robinson earned university letters in four sports his first year at Pasadena.

Off the playing field Jackie was still the same mischievous boy he had been as a young kid throwing acorns at his schoolmates. Even though he was now a college man, he still liked to pull pranks on friends. One classmate recalled that if Robinson saw a friend eating a snack at the movies, "he might go up and knock it out of his hand and not say a thing about it. He was just devilish that way. . . . Everything was a lot of fun to Jack."

Even though Robinson enjoyed college life, he still had to come to terms with prejudice. Some members of the football team weren't used to playing with blacks. There was some hostility at first, but Robinson worked with the coach and his teammates to overcome the problem. On road trips there were different issues. On one trip to Sacramento with the track team Robinson was refused service in a restaurant. In a show of support, almost the entire team rose in unison and walked out of the restaurant, leaving behind one lone Oklahoman teammate. Another time in Phoenix, Robinson and the other black players on the team weren't allowed into a hotel, but were shown to separate quarters. Enraged at the treatment shown them, the players refused the rooms. Instead, they stayed up all night in the lobby.

❝*That isn't stealing. It's grand larceny.***❞**

—RUBE SAMUELSEN,
SPORTSWRITER, COMMENTING ON ROBINSON'S BASE STEALING

In his second year at Pasadena, Robinson's fame grew. On May 7, 1938, he had a particularly outstanding day. At a track meet for the Southern California Junior Track Championships, Robinson competed in the long jump. The long jump was a favorite of Robinson's. He once described what the experience of jumping was like: "You [toe] the line and spring forward with all your strength. Then you jump—you really try to jump off the earth and your legs churn the air like you wanted to reach the moon. Then you come down to earth in soft sand and you have to remember to fall forward so that there are no marks behind the backs of your heels."

That particular day, his brother Mack's record must have been on his mind. Mack held the national college record for the event. In the long jump an athlete has three tries. The longest jump is the one that counts. Robinson fouled his first jump. His second jump landed him in second place. Robinson knew if he had any hope of breaking the record, he had to do it on his last try. He took off down the runway, arms pumping, and jumped. He landed feetfirst in the sandpit, not knowing if the record was his. The judges came with their tape measures and checked it out. Robinson had jumped twenty-five feet, six and a half inches, breaking the record set by his older brother and winning the meet.

Such an accomplishment would have been more than enough for most athletes, but Robinson wasn't finished that day. After the track meet Robinson jumped in a friend's car and headed for Glendale, forty miles away. During the car ride he changed into his baseball uniform. The Bulldogs, Robinson's baseball team, were playing against Glendale Junior College in a championship game. Arriving late, Robinson still managed a hit and a stolen base, helping to clinch his team's victory. Robinson's performance that day added to his growing legend.

Robinson had entered Pasadena Junior College a skinny boy, weighing only 135 pounds. After two years at Pasadena his body had filled out. By age twenty he was 175 pounds and he had reached his full height, just under six feet. From playing football and other sports, his body had become more muscular. He might have entered junior college a boy, but he was walking out a man.

Not many colleges had been interested in Robinson when he graduated from high school, but all that changed as he prepared to leave Pasadena. Many major universities now offered him scholarships. Robinson considered a few of them, but in the end he decided to accept the University of California at Los Angeles (UCLA). Robinson liked UCLA for several reasons. Tuition was free, and the school was within commuting distance of his home. Also, he knew that if he played for UCLA, he would be sure to play in games, not be a benchwarmer.

The summer between junior and senior college was a traumatic one for Robinson. His older brother Frank Robinson was killed in a motorcycle accident. When Robinson heard the news, he rushed to the hospital where Frank had been taken, unconscious. He was badly injured and did not survive the night. Frank had been one of Jackie's biggest supporters.

Robinson called him "my greatest fan." Frank had always helped scout out players on opposing teams for Robinson. He also attended all of his younger brother's games, cheering loudly in the stands. Robinson was deeply shaken by Frank's death. "It was hard to believe he was gone," Robinson wrote, "hard to believe I would no longer have his support."

Robinson's grief over his brother was still fresh when he became involved in a disturbing incident. Robinson and some friends were riding home from a softball game when a passing driver, seeing the group of young black men, hurled racial insults at them. Robinson, always ready to defend himself, answered the man back. The two cars stopped and a crowd gathered. Before long a police officer arrived. He looked at the crowd of young blacks and decided that they had started the trouble. Most of the crowd began slipping away, but not Robinson. Knowing he had done nothing wrong, he was unwilling to back down. He was arrested and jailed overnight, charged with resisting arrest and blocking traffic. When the case came to trial, he was fined $50. Although in the end his arrest did not prove serious, Robinson was left with the knowledge that if he were white, he would never have been arrested at all.

Deciding to put his terrible summer behind him, Robinson began classes that fall at UCLA. As he had done at Pasadena, he played on four teams: football, basketball, baseball, and track.

THE TRAINING TABLE

At UCLA, Robinson tried out for the baseball team and played shortstop, but not with the success he enjoyed in football and basketball. Why did Robinson perform so poorly? One reason may be that the football and basketball programs provided their players with food during the playing season—meals that were eaten at the "training table." Baseball players didn't enjoy this perk.

He lettered in all four sports, making history by becoming UCLA's first player to do so.

But Robinson did not enjoy his college days at UCLA the way he had at Pasadena. To his teammates he seemed withdrawn and at times unfriendly. Perhaps his brother's death and his recent brush with the law caused Robinson to lose a bit of his carefree attitude. He wasn't so aloof, though, that he didn't notice pretty women like Rachel Isum, a classmate at UCLA. Rachel, a freshman, was studying to be a nurse, and Robinson often saw her with her nose buried in a book. He wanted very much to meet her, but Robinson had always been shy with girls and he could never summon up enough courage to introduce himself to her.

One day, he confessed his attraction to Rachel to his friend Ray Bartlett. Ray didn't know Rachel, either, but he wasn't shy around the ladies. He marched Robinson up to Rachel and introduced his friend to her. Rachel later confessed to Robinson that she had been quite aware of who Jackie Robinson was. She had even once seen him play football in high school and had thought he was pretty full of himself. But as she got to know the real Jackie Robinson, Rachel found that she liked him very much. The two began dating, and in a very short time they fell in love.

❝Geez, if that kid was white I'd sign him right now.❞
—JIMMY DYKES,
WHITE SOX MANAGER

Although tuition was free at UCLA and Robinson had a scholarship for additional expenses, money was still a problem. During his years in college Robinson held a number of part-time jobs. He worked as a valet and as a busboy to earn extra money. By 1941, Robinson, dissatisfied with college, was eager to get on with his life. He believed that "no amount of education would help a black man get a job." He also wanted to help support his mother. He hoped to get a coaching position somewhere. Despite objections from Mallie and Rachel, he quit UCLA just a few months before graduation. Robinson, now twenty-two, was ready to face his future.

Chapter Four

You're in the Army Now

After college Robinson found work as an athletic director at a training camp for disadvantaged children in Atascadero, California. Robinson organized sports activities and supervised the kids' free time. He also played shortstop on the camp's baseball team. He enjoyed the job and probably was aware that he, once on the verge of being a juvenile delinquent, was now in a position of authority to help children like himself. He realized that he "had been no different than many of these kids, who would make good if given half a chance." By summer, though, the camp disbanded permanently and Robinson was without a job.

Luckily another opportunity soon presented itself. The Honolulu Bears, a semiprofessional football team in Hawaii, offered him a spot on the team. That September, Robinson sailed to Honolulu, where he and a teammate shared a duplex apartment. Robinson did his best for the team but injured his ankle early on in the season. He continued to play but because of his hurt ankle did not perform well. By the last game he was eager to return home and see Rachel and his family.

On December 5, 1941, Robinson boarded the *Lurline* for the journey back to California. Three days later, while playing cards with fellow passengers, he noticed crewmen with paint cans hurriedly painting the ship's windows black. Robinson must have wondered what was going on. He soon found out. The captain ordered everyone on deck and informed them that the day before, the Japanese had bombed Pearl Harbor. The country was at war.

BASEBALL DURING WORLD WAR II

World War II had a major effect on baseball. Over 500 major leaguers and 3,500 minor leaguers went to war. Many people thought that the shortage of players would mean that blacks would finally be allowed to play. This didn't happen. Instead, less talented players filled in for the stars.

Robinson received his draft notice in March and reported to the army. Like many men at that time, he was willing to do

> **❝**I'm not concerned with your liking or disliking me. . . .
> All I ask is that you respect me as a human being.**❞**
>
> —JACKIE ROBINSON

his part for his country. After being given a physical examination, he was sent for thirteen weeks of basic training at Fort Riley, Kansas. Robinson performed well at boot camp. He was rated an excellent marksman on the gunnery range, and his character was likewise rated excellent. Because of this, Robinson decided to enroll in Officer Candidate School (OCS) and become an officer. He sent in his application. It was rejected without an explanation. Robinson suspected he knew the reason. Blacks were not considered officer material. As he usually did, Robinson didn't take this news lying down. He fought back— with a fighter.

Joe Louis, the heavyweight boxing champion and a black man, was also stationed at Fort Riley. At the peak of his fame, the fighter befriended Robinson. The two men often played golf together and went out horseback riding. Robinson told Louis about the rejection of his application and asked for his help. Louis used his influence, and after a few highly placed phone calls, Robinson's application was accepted.

With thirteen weeks of training under his belt, Robinson

graduated from OCS and became a second lieutenant in the U.S. Army. Jack stood tall as the gold bars were pinned on his cavalry uniform. At that time the armed forces weren't integrated. There were separate facilities for white and black soldiers. They ate in separate quarters, slept in separate quarters, and even had to use separate bathrooms. Robinson, as an officer, was assigned as a morale officer to an all-black unit of soldiers. By all accounts he was a good officer and his men liked and respected him. When Robinson's men complained that while there were plenty of seats in the post exchange most were reserved for whites only, Robinson quickly telephoned a superior officer to see about getting more chairs for his men. The officer, who did not know that Robinson was black, wasn't sympathetic. He asked Robinson if he would want his wife sitting next to a black person. Only he didn't use the term "black person," but a much more insulting word. Robinson exploded. In the office where he worked, typewriters stopped. People froze as they heard him tell the officer exactly what he thought of his despicable views. A few days after the phone call, more seats suddenly became available for black soldiers.

Robinson won that battle, but he lost others. When he went to try out for the Fort Riley baseball team, the coach cruelly told him that as a black man he wasn't allowed to join. Pete Reiser, who would later play with Robinson on the Brooklyn

Dodgers, witnessed Robinson's rejection: "One day we were out at the field practicing, when a Negro lieutenant came out for the team. An officer told him, 'You have to play with the colored team.' That was a joke. There was no colored team. The black lieutenant didn't speak. He stood there for a while, watched us work out, and then he turned and walked away. . . . That was the first time I saw Jackie Robinson. I can still see him slowly walking away."

While baseball didn't want him, football did. He was invited to join the fort's team. He practiced with the squad, but right before the season's start he was given two weeks' leave. The leave was surprising because he hadn't requested it. Robinson soon found out why he had been sent away. The team's first game was against the University of Missouri. Missouri had made it known that they would not play football with any team that had a black player on it. Robinson went on leave. When he returned, he resigned. He would not play for a team that didn't allow him to play in all of its games.

Robinson and some other officers were later transferred to the 761st tank battalion at Fort Hood, Texas. Robinson, however, had been trained in the cavalry. He knew horses, not tanks. Facing his men, he decided that honesty was the best policy. Instead of trying to bluff his way through, he admitted that he didn't know a thing about tanks. He then asked them

> **❝There's not an American in this country free until every one of us is free.❞**
>
> —JACKIE ROBINSON

to help him out in "this unusual situation." Later, Robinson said that his decision "turned out to be one of the smartest things I ever did." The men respected his candor and served him well. His commanding officer, Colonel Paul Bates, also thought highly of Robinson.

It was a good thing Bates valued Robinson. Before the year was over, Jackie would need his superior's full support. On July 6, 1944, Robinson became involved in a serious dispute that almost got him kicked out of the army. Boarding a camp bus, he recognized the wife of a fellow officer and went to sit by her. The two began chatting. Suddenly the bus driver ordered Robinson to the back of the bus. At that time in Texas, buses were segregated. Blacks were supposed to sit at the back of buses so that whites could have the front to themselves. Robinson knew this. He also knew that the army had banned segregated seating on all its bases. This ruling had come about after Joe Louis and another famous fighter, Ray Robinson, had challenged the rules at a bus depot in Alabama. Jackie Robinson, once again not backing down from a challenge, refused.

The bus driver insisted that Robinson move to the back. If he didn't, he would be in big trouble when the bus reached the station. Robinson wasn't afraid of trouble. He felt that as a black man he was entitled to ride where he wanted. He was sure that the army would back him up.

When the bus arrived at the bus station, the military police were waiting. After questioning him and other witnesses, Robinson was put under house arrest. At his court-martial trial, Colonel Bates and others testified to Robinson's good character, and witnesses on the bus supported Robinson's version of events. After a trial that lasted four hours, he was cleared of all charges.

Although he had been found innocent, Robinson was now viewed as a troublemaker by the army. He was transferred to Camp Breckinridge, Kentucky, and then to Camp Wheeler, Georgia. At last, on November 28, 1944, Robinson was granted an honorable discharge from the army and was able to return home to California.

A civilian once again, one of Robinson's first orders of business was finding a job. He applied for a number of coaching positions, but when he arrived for interviews, he was always told that the job was filled. Robinson must have suspected that his skin color played a part in his rejections. While still in the army, Robinson had presented Rachel with an engagement ring. Without a job or the prospect of one, Robinson knew there was no way they could afford to get married.

After many more interviews, he was at last offered a position teaching physical education at an African American college in Texas. Enrollment was small, only about 300 students. When Robinson put out a call for basketball tryouts, only seven men showed up. Still, Robinson put all his energies into coaching the team. To inspire his players, he put his many medals and trophies on display. The team didn't win many games, but they did manage to beat the defending champions in a 61–59 game. Unfortunately, although Robinson enjoyed teaching, the pay at the college wasn't much.

While at Camp Breckinridge, Robinson had met a soldier who had once played for the Kansas City Monarchs, a baseball team in the Negro Leagues. This player had advised Robinson to think about a career there. The war had left the leagues short of talent. They would welcome players like Robinson. Robinson took his advice and wrote a letter to the Monarchs, requesting a job. That spring Robinson joined the Monarchs for spring training. His salary was $400 a month. That was a good deal of money to Robinson, and he hoped to save some. Maybe he could even save enough so that he and Rachel could marry and start a family.

Chapter Five

Kansas City, Here I Come

Although he was now a shortstop with the Monarchs, Robinson was still divided about being in the Negro Leagues. The Negro Leagues were separate leagues made up entirely of black players. They had come about after blacks were banned from organized baseball in the nineteenth century. In 1920 Andrew Foster, a former pitcher, put together a new league in which blacks would have an opportunity to play. Robinson didn't like segregation in any shape or form. He felt that baseball teams should be open to all players, no matter what their color. On the other hand, he recognized that the Negro Leagues gave blacks a chance to play baseball that otherwise they would never have.

Robinson enjoyed being back on the field, but he didn't enjoy the lifestyle that went along with being a player in the Negro Leagues. Games were played year-round—there was no off season. There were times when the team had to play two doubleheaders on the same day. In addition, the Monarchs, like all black teams, traveled from town to town in uncomfortable buses. Most hotels didn't accept blacks, so players had no choice but to sleep in the bus for the night. Because many restaurants refused to serve blacks, meals were usually take-out ones, again eaten on the dreaded bus. Rest rooms were another problem. Most of the time players used the rest rooms in gas stations. A few times the team was refused their use. Once Robinson became so enraged that he demanded the attendant stop filling the bus with gas. Why should the team give the station their money if they weren't allowed common courtesies? After that, the Monarchs had a new policy: If a station didn't allow players to use the rest rooms, the team went elsewhere for gas.

❝A pretty miserable way to make a buck.❞

—JACKIE ROBINSON
ON PLAYING BASEBALL IN THE NEGRO LEAGUES

Robinson might not have been all that impressed with the Negro Leagues, but the leagues weren't all that impressed with him, either—at least not at first. Jimmie Crutchfield, a player for the Pittsburgh Crawfords, remembered the first time he saw

Robinson play. Robinson hadn't played ball for five years when he first joined the Monarchs, and he wasn't yet in top physical form. Crutchfield thought Robinson was out of shape and clumsy. "I thought the Monarchs had him just for a publicity stunt because he had been so great in college." Crutchfield soon learned better. "We were playing an exhibition game in Houston, Texas, and Jackie hit a ball between the third baseman and the bag down the left-field line. Our left fielder ran over and got the ball quickly and wheeled it into second. But Jackie was standing on the bag. He was already there. I knew right then the guy could move. We were together for about six or seven games that spring, and during that time we couldn't get him out."

The Negro Leagues might not have held much attraction for Robinson, but the major leagues certainly did. Not long after he became a Monarch, Robinson was invited to try out for the Boston Red Sox. Robinson suspected that the offer wasn't a serious one, and he was right. The Red Sox had no intention of hiring him. Boston politicians were pressuring the Red Sox to integrate the team. To appease these politicians, the Red Sox agreed to try out three players from the Negro Leagues. Robinson and the other two players went to Fenway Park and fielded, threw to bases, and hit balls. According to reporters who witnessed his play, Robinson was clearly the most striking of the three. Even the Red Sox were impressed. Joe Cronin, manager of the Red Sox, watched the tryout from a secluded spot. He later stated, "If I had that guy on my club, we'd be a world beater." In spite of the praise, neither Robinson nor the other two players ever heard back from the Red Sox. Robinson wasn't surprised.

Even though his tryout hadn't panned out, Robinson decided that he was through with the Negro Leagues. He was unhappy with the hard conditions, and he missed Rachel, whom he rarely saw since he was so often on the road. He told the Monarchs owner, J. L. Wilkinson, that he wanted to quit. Wilkinson gave him a raise in pay and talked him into staying with the team.

Robinson didn't exactly fit in with his new teammates. First of all, he was college educated, which many of his fellow Monarchs weren't. Second, Robinson believed strongly in self-discipline. He didn't drink or swear or party into the wee hours. For all these reasons, Robinson sometimes felt like an outsider among his teammates.

Still, some of the Monarchs, especially the older players, did take Jackie under their wing. Teammate Cool Papa Bell gave Robinson lessons in base stealing. In the Negro Leagues players used tactics called trickeration to steal bases. A player would dance on and off a base, unnerving the pitcher and causing him either to balk or to let the player steal a base. The lessons in trickeration must have been good ones because when he reached the major leagues, Robinson became famous for his base stealing. Robinson also learned plenty about baseball in the "skull sessions" that took place after a game. Win or lose, the team would talk about the game, what had taken place on the field, what they could have done differently, what they didn't do.

THE KANSAS CITY MONARCHS

The Kansas City Monarchs were a first-class baseball team, the New York Yankees of the Negro Leagues. They possessed a distinguished history, winning more than a dozen championships. Some of the finest players in black baseball were Monarchs, including the legendary Satchel Paige, Cool Papa Bell, and Norman "Turkey" Stearnes. After Jackie Robinson broke baseball's color barrier, the Monarchs sent more players into the major leagues than any other team in the Negro Leagues.

With such talented players to watch and learn from, Robinson's game improved dramatically. At midseason he was selected to play in the East-West All-Star game in Chicago. Official stats weren't kept in the Negro Leagues, but it's been calculated that Robinson hit .350 that season. Robinson himself complained, "I could never figure out my batting average because so many games did not count in the league statistics. . . . Nobody knew for sure."

He wasn't the fastest runner on the team, but he was still extremely quick. And his teammates all agreed that he was a great bunter. They also agreed that Robinson had "brains," one of the reasons he was such a great baseball player. "Tell him something once and you never had to tell him again; he'd pick your brains and you'd never even know it," one player remarked.

Robinson was making great strides as a player, but he was still unhappy playing with the Monarchs. Unknown to him, scouts were following his progress. And not just any scouts, but scouts for the Brooklyn Dodgers. Wesley Branch Rickey, the new president of the Dodgers, had big plans under way. Plans that he wanted to keep secret, at least at first. Rickey wanted to sign a black player and integrate professional baseball. He had both personal and professional reasons for wanting to do so. As the president of the Dodgers, Rickey, like all presidents, wanted his team to win. World War II had brought about a shortage of talent. Rickey felt that the many excellent players in the black leagues could bring his team a championship.

But Rickey had another, more personal reason for wanting to integrate baseball. In 1904 Rickey, just starting out in base-ball, was a coach of a college baseball team. One of his best players was a young black man named Charles Thomas. While on the road, the team checked into a hotel. Thomas, because he was black, was denied a room. Rickey talked management into letting Thomas share his room, and a cot was placed next to his bed. That night Rickey witnessed Thomas sobbing at his mistreatment and overheard him cursing his dark skin and wishing he could rub it off. This scene deeply affected Rickey, who never forgot it. He vowed "that I would always do whatever I could to see that other Americans did not have to face the bitter humiliation that was heaped upon Charles Thomas." Now, over forty years later, Rickey would have that chance.

What a ballplayer! Too bad he's the wrong color.

—HUGH DUFFY, SCOUT

Rickey, however, didn't want just any black player. In order for his "great experiment" to work, he needed a special person. Obviously he needed a superb ballplayer. That went without saying. But the person selected would have to be more than just a great ballplayer. He'd have to be someone who could withstand the terrible treatment he was sure to receive. First, though, Rickey concentrated on finding top ballplayers. He sent out his scouts to look for the best black athletes in the Negro

Leagues. When evaluating a prospect, the scouts had to con-sider three things: Could the player run? Could he throw? Could he hit with power? The scouts returned with their reports. One name was at the top of all three lists: Jackie Robinson.

Chapter Six

The Great Experiment Begins

On August 28, 1945, Robinson entered Branch Rickey's Brooklyn office at 215 Montague Street. With him was Clyde Sukeforth, a Dodger scout. Four days earlier Sukeforth had convinced Robinson to miss a few games with the Monarchs in order to meet with Rickey. Robinson thought he was in Brooklyn to discuss his joining the Brown Dodgers, an all-black team that Rickey was supposedly starting. In fact, the Brown Dodgers were fictional. Rickey had invented the team to disguise his real intentions. He was afraid that if the press discovered that he wanted to hire a black player, his great experiment would end before it had ever begun.

The wood-paneled office was dark and richly furnished with stuffed leather chairs. A fish tank stood in a corner. Perhaps Robinson noted that one of the oil portraits hanging on the wall was of Abraham Lincoln. Behind a mahogany desk sat

Branch Rickey. He stood when Robinson and Sukeforth entered the room, and the two men shook hands. The general manager and president of the Brooklyn Dodgers was a bulky man with bushy eyebrows and wire spectacles. Although the office was hot, he wore a jacket and a bow tie. After shaking hands, the two men stared at each other, as if taking each other's measure. Sukeforth later said that the "air in the office was electric."

In his deep, booming voice, one of the first questions Rickey asked Robinson was, "Do you have a girl?" Robinson was surprised. He thought the question was nobody's business but his own. However, he explained to Rickey about Rachel and his plans to marry her. Rickey's response was to say Robinson might want to call Rachel—that "there are times when a man needs a woman by his side."

Robinson's heart began to beat faster. All along he had suspected that Rickey hadn't brought him to New York to talk about the Brown Dodgers. Rickey, anticipating this reaction, asked Robinson if he knew why he had sent for him. Robinson

Branch Rickey's search to find the right man to integrate baseball cost the Brooklyn Dodger organization $25,000.

related what Clyde Sukeforth had told him about the Brown Dodgers. Rickey chuckled. "That's what he was supposed to tell you." Then he told Robinson the real reason for the meeting. He wanted Robinson to play in the major leagues, starting out with the Montreal Royals, a farm club, and eventually, with luck, playing as a Brooklyn Dodger.

Robinson sat in the plush leather chair, speechless. Whatever he had expected, it wasn't this. To have a chance to play in the major leagues, to finally show everyone what he was capable of, was a dream come true. Puzzled by Robinson's silence, Rickey leaned forward. "Do you think you can do it?" he demanded. Sukeforth remembered the moment. "Jack waited, and waited, and waited before answering. . . . We were all just looking at him." Finally he responded. "Yes," he said.

Rickey wasn't through, though. He wanted to make sure that Robinson knew what he was getting himself into. Would Robinson be able to stand up to all the abuse that was sure to come his way? "I know you're a good ballplayer," Rickey told him. "What I don't know is whether you have the guts."

This remark got to Robinson. Was Rickey questioning his manhood? Was he calling him a coward? Robinson felt his temper build and he was about to explode when Rickey explained, "I'm looking for a ballplayer with guts enough not to fight back."

Robinson hadn't thought about this side of things. All his life, from the time he was eight years old and had thrown rocks at his abusive neighbor, he had stood up for himself. In high school and college he had never let others push him around. In the army he had fought for his men and had refused to move to the back of the bus. Did he possess the courage to do nothing?

❝They didn't make a mistake by signing Robinson. They couldn't have picked a better man.❞

—SATCHEL PAIGE

Rickey continued, "We can't fight our way through this, Robinson. We've got no army. There's virtually nobody on our side. No owners, no umpires, very few newspapermen. And I'm afraid that many fans will be hostile. We'll be in a tough position. We can win only if we can convince the world that I'm doing this because you're a great ballplayer and a fine gentleman."

Then he asked Robinson the question he had asked earlier. This time he said each word slowly and carefully. "Have you got the guts to play the game no matter what happens?"

"I think I can play the game, Mr. Rickey," Robinson responded.

What happened next must have surprised Robinson. Before his astonished eyes, Rickey began to act out some of the situations Robinson would face. First Rickey was a room clerk denying him service, then a waiter insulting him in a restaurant, then a haughty railroad conductor. He took off his jacket and became a ballplayer, swinging his pudgy fists at Robinson's face. He called Robinson every insult he could think of, in language that was "almost unendurable."

When he was finished, Robinson was shaken. Would he be able to turn the other cheek, as Rickey had asked of him? He couldn't be positive, but he knew that he had to try. He later said, "I had to do it for many reasons. For black youth, for my mother, for Rae, for myself. I had already begun to feel I had to do it for Branch Rickey."

BRANCH RICKEY AND THE FARM SYSTEM

Aside from his role in integrating baseball, Branch Rickey was also responsible for creating baseball's farm system. The farm system develops young and inexperienced players in minor league teams and grooms them for playing in the major leagues. That was Rickey's proposition to Jackie Robinson. Robinson would start out as a Montreal Royal, one of the Brooklyn Dodgers' minor league teams, and, once he proved himself, work his way up to the major leagues.

The meeting with Rickey lasted over two hours. At the end, Robinson signed an agreement binding him to the Brooklyn Dodgers. Once he signed the contract, he would receive a $3,500 bonus and a $600-a-month salary. Rickey had one last request to make. Except for Rachel and his mother, Robinson was to tell no one of their deal.

Robinson kept his promise. The Monarchs, unhappy with his sudden, unexplained trip to New York, lectured Robinson about his absence and advised him to shape up. Already unhappy with life in the Negro Leagues, Robinson quit the team and returned to California.

On October 23, 1945, Robinson signed a contract to play organized baseball with the Montreal Royals. At a press conference Robinson, even though he was "nervous as the devil," calmly answered reporters' questions. "I can only say," he told them, "I'll do my very best to come through in every manner."

Public reaction was swift. Many people were supportive. "I guarantee if Jackie Robinson hits homers and plays a whale of a game for Montreal, the fans will lose sight of his color," one sportswriter wrote. Others, however, opposed the deal. "Robinson is a one thousand-to-one shot to make the grade," Jimmy Powers, a *New York Daily News* columnist, wrote. Everyone, it seemed, had an opinion. Would Robinson make fans forget his color, or was he a thousand-to-one shot, as predicted?

Chapter Seven

A Royal Man

On March 2, 1946, Jackie and Rachel Robinson stepped off a Greyhound bus after thirty-six hours of travel. Husband and wife now, the couple had headed to Daytona Beach, Florida, after their honeymoon so that Robinson could attend the Royals' spring training. The trip was horrible. Rachel had never traveled in the South and wasn't used to the way blacks were treated there. In New Orleans they had to give up their airline seats to military officials. In Pensacola, Florida, they were bumped again, this time for a white couple. Fed up with the airlines, they decided to take a bus the rest of the way. On the bus they sat crowded at the back. In front of them, in the whites-only section, were plenty of available seats. Robinson was upset, but he knew better than to make a scene. Instead he and Rachel endured their discomfort quietly.

Daytona Beach, which Branch Rickey had chosen as his

A ROYAL WEDDING

In February 1946 Jackie Roosevelt Robinson married
Rachel Isum in a ceremony that didn't go smoothly. The
best man misplaced the ring. Going back down the aisle,
an elated Robinson left his bride to whoop and holler with
his old pals from the Pepper Street Gang, leaving Rachel to
walk the rest of the way by herself. Then, ready to
leave the reception, the newlyweds discovered that the
Pepper Street Gang had made off with their car as a joke,
and the couple had to wait several hours until it was
returned. At last they made it to the hotel to start their
honeymoon, only to find that Robinson had forgotten to
make a reservation there.

spring-training base, was a liberal community and one of the few places that welcomed Robinson. Perhaps one of the reasons was that the city looked forward to the extra money that having such a team would bring. But the nearby town of Sanford, where the Royals also practiced spring training, was downright hostile to him. Robinson reported to Sanford for the first day of training on March 4, dressed in his gray Royal uniform. Around the entrance to the field stood an angry, menacing crowd. In order to get inside, Robinson had to squeeze through a hole in the fence.

Once safely inside, he faced another challenge. On the field milled the ballplayers, all white. As the men practiced their fielding, running, and throwing, they kept up a steady hum of chatter. When Robinson stepped onto the field, there was silence. "It seemed that every one of those men stopped suddenly in his tracks and that four hundred eyes were trained on . . . me," Robinson said.

❝I just mean to do the best I can.❞

—JACKIE ROBINSON

Reporters were suddenly upon him, bombarding him with questions. One asked him if he would be able to get along with his fellow players. "I've gotten along with white boys in high school, at Pasadena, at UCLA, and in the army," Robinson replied. "I don't see why these should be any different." Another reporter asked what he would do if one of the pitchers threw at his head. Robinson had a quick reply to that one. "I'd duck!" By the time the last reporter had left, there was no doubt that Robinson knew how to handle the press.

Robinson was then introduced to the new manager of the Montreal Royals, Clay Hopper. Hopper, a southern man, had made it very clear that he didn't want Robinson on his team. He had pleaded with Rickey not to sign Robinson. He told him, "I'm white and I've lived in Mississippi all my life. If you do this, you're going to force me to move my family out of Mississippi." In spite of the way he felt, however, Hopper was a professional. He was cordial to Robinson, and the two men shook hands.

Robinson worked hard at practice for the next two days, trying to lose some of the extra weight he had put on over the winter. Then, without warning, Robinson was quickly hustled out of town. Later he learned why. A large number of the town's citizens had called on the mayor, demanding that Robinson leave. Rickey decided that remaining in Sanford was no longer safe, so the team returned to Daytona.

Back in Daytona, Robinson didn't perform well. Perhaps the uproar of the past few days hung heavily on him. Robinson very much wanted to show his teammates, Rickey, and the rest of the world what he was capable of. He was frustrated by his performance and even more frustrated when he injured his throwing arm. In this troubling time Rickey supported him. He would tell Robinson not to worry about his arm, it would get better, and encouraged him to be bold and daring. Robinson appreciated his support, and the two men grew closer.

While Robinson had Rickey's confidence and respect, the same couldn't be said of his teammates. It wasn't as if the

Royals were hostile to Robinson, they just weren't particularly friendly. Robinson felt excluded, in part, because he didn't room with the rest of the players. The hotel where the Royals stayed didn't allow blacks. Instead he and Rachel roomed with a black family. But as time passed, some players warmed up to Robinson, and a few actually went out of their way to help the new player. Lou Rochelli was Robinson's rival for third base, yet he frequently gave the new player tips. Al Campanis helped Robinson work on his double plays. He also was the only player to sit and eat with Robinson on road trips.

As Robinson and the Royals got used to one another, spring training drew to a close. On March 17 Robinson nervously waited for his name to be called in the season's first exhibition game. The Royals were playing against their parent team, the Dodgers. Four thousand people crammed into the ballpark, a thousand of them blacks eager to see Robinson perform. His name called at last, Robinson heard mostly the cheers—he had to strain to catch the few scattered boos. Although he went hitless, he stole a base and scored a run.

Soon after, Robinson fell into a slump. As most ballplayers know, there isn't much you can do about a slump. You just continue to play your best, and in time the slump ends. For Robinson, though, the pressure was enormous. Every day without a hit made him more afraid that he would be cut from the team.

Rickey, however, was unconcerned about his star player's slump. "He'll hit," Rickey promised, "and he'll be quite a ballplayer. I'm sure of that." Perhaps Rickey's confidence in him took some of the pressure off because by the end of March, Robinson was hitting again.

Unfortunately new troubles followed. Many towns, not wanting blacks to play in their ballparks, canceled exhibition games. Some towns came straight out with the reason why—they didn't want black players on their fields. Other towns offered feeble excuses. One town claimed its stadium lights weren't working. Since the scheduled game was to be played in the daytime, it wasn't a very believable excuse. In Sanford, Robinson played only two innings before the chief of police ordered Hopper to remove him from the game. He wasn't even allowed to sit on the bench. He had to leave the ballpark.

Rickey refused to give in to these strong-arm tactics. He knew what the towns and the other teams wanted. They wanted him to take Robinson off the team. Rickey wouldn't budge. If Jackie Robinson didn't play, then the Royals didn't play.

On opening day of the regular season against the Jersey City Giants, Jackie Robinson had an almost perfect game. The Royals went on to sweep the three-game series. Robinson was off to a fantastic start as a Royal. The next series against the Baltimore Orioles, though, was a setback. Baltimore, a city below the Mason-Dixon line, was hostile to Robinson, and the white fans abused him.

But it wasn't only the fans who tormented Robinson. Many players on opposing teams had it in for him. They slid into second base with their spikes high, often wounding him. When he faced pitchers, they aimed for his head. Once in Syracuse, as Robinson stood at the plate getting ready to hit, a player tossed a black cat from the dugout onto the field. "Hey, Jackie," he yelled, "there's your cousin." The umpire called time, and the cat was rescued. Afterward Robinson scored on a single to center. As he trotted past the Syracuse dugout, he shouted, "I guess my cousin's pretty happy now."

Life as a Royal was tough for Robinson, and he was always glad when the team headed home, back to Montreal. The reception he received in this Canadian city was very different from what he received on the road. Montreal loved Jackie Robinson, and the feeling was mutual. He and Rachel had found an apartment in the French-speaking part of the city, where the newlyweds were made to feel very much at home. Even though they couldn't speak a word of French, they felt their neighbors' warmth. At the games the Montreal fans cheered their hearts out for Robinson and the rest of the Royals. "I owe more to Canadians than they'll ever know," he said. "In my baseball career they were the first to make me feel my natural self."

> **❝***I know now that dreams do come true.***❞**
>
> —JACKIE ROBINSON

Robinson now began to get into his stride. As the season progressed, he led the league in hitting. His average of .349 set a team record. He scored 113 runs, more than anyone else in the league, and, with forty stolen bases, was second in the league. His playing did not go unnoticed. "I'd like to have nine Robinsons," Bruno Betzel, manager of the Jersey City Giants, declared. At the end of the regular season Robinson received a great honor when he was named the league's most valuable player (MVP).

After the team won the play-offs, they traveled to Kentucky to face the Louisville Colonels in the minor leagues' Little World Series. The Royals were bringing integrated baseball to Louisville for the first time. Many blacks were eager to see Robinson play. The Colonels, though, limited the number of tickets black fans could buy. Many black fans climbed to high points outside the stadium to catch a glimpse of Robinson.

The white fans who filled the majority of the seats unleashed their hatred at Robinson. He suffered some of the worst abuse he had come across. The experience unnerved

Classmates.com

Jackie as he appears in
his high-school yearbook

UCLA's first student athlete
to earn varsity letters in
four different sports, Jackie
plays quarterback here for
his football team at UCLA.

© Bettmann/CORBIS

© AP Wide World Photos

The first African American to play in the major leagues, Jackie makes history by signing with the Montreal Royals on October 23, 1945.

Jackie's young fans bridge the color gap.

© Bettmann/CORBIS

© AP Wide World Photos

As he prepares to play his first game in Philadelphia for the Brooklyn Dodgers, Jackie poses with Phillies manager Ben Chapman.

© Bettmann/CORBIS

Jackie slides into second, knocking Yankee Phil Rizzuto off his feet in the sixth game of the 1947 World Series.

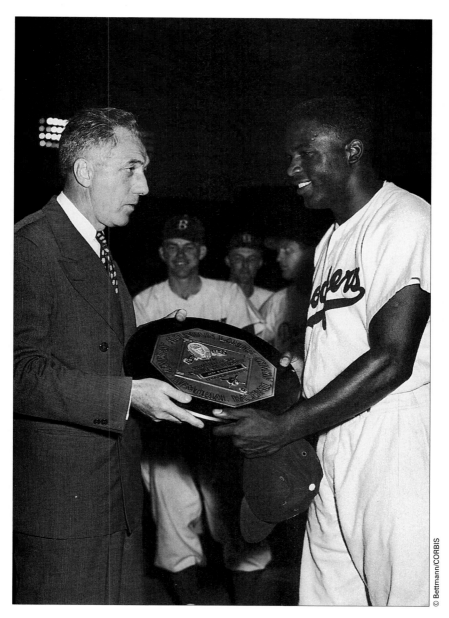

Jackie receives the Most Valuable Player award for the 1949 season.

© Bettmann/CORBIS

© Bettmann/CORBIS

The Dodgers rush the mound after winning the 1955 World Series.

© AP Wide World Photos

Jackie with his family at their home in Stamford, Connecticut, in February 1962

© Bettmann/CORBIS

Jackie proudly displays his plaque after he is inducted into the National Baseball Hall of Fame in Cooperstown, New York, on July 23, 1962.

him, and he didn't play his best. The Royals played three games in Louisville, and Robinson hit only one for eleven. Robinson later recalled that the worse he played, "the more vicious that howling mob in the stands became. I had been booed pretty soundly before, but nothing like this. A torrent of mass hatred burst from the stands with virtually every move I made."

The Royals lost two of the three games. Then the series went to Montreal to play the remaining games. In order to win the World Series, the Royals had to win three of four games. The Montreal fans knew what had happened in Louisville. When the Colonels arrived to play in the ballpark, they were soundly booed. The loyalty of the Montreal fans cheered Robinson, and his play improved. In the remaining games he had seven hits. In the fifth game Louisville had tied the game. Robinson responded by hitting a triple.

Football was the next sport to break the color barrier. In March 1946 the Los Angeles Rams signed Kenny Washington.

On October 4, 1946, the Royals defeated the Colonels and won the championship. The Montreal fans exploded onto the field, overjoyed. Hoisting Robinson onto their shoulders, they carried him around, singing songs and cheering loudly. In the locker room Hopper, the man who hadn't wanted Robinson to play on his team, came over and shook his hand. "You're a great ballplayer and a fine gentleman," he told his star player. "It's been wonderful having you on the team."

Having changed into his street clothes and eager to catch a plane, Robinson found a large crowd waiting for him. The crowd surged around him, wanting to touch their hero, in the process almost ripping the clothes from his back. Robinson at last broke away and ran down the street, the crowd at his heels. A reporter wrote of the scene, "It was probably the only day in history that a black man ran from a white mob with love instead of lynching on its mind."

Chapter | Eight

Rookie of the Year

When the new year arrived, Robinson, still a Royal, was waiting for the call that would send him to the Dodgers. Would it ever come? Other minor league top hitters had been promoted to the majors; why not Robinson? Although Branch Rickey very much wanted Robinson to be a Dodger, he didn't want to rush the matter. He felt that when the Dodgers saw how good Robinson was, they would want him on their team. He told a reporter, "If Robinson merits being with the Dodgers, I'd prefer to have the players want him, rather than force him on the players. I want Robinson to have the fairest chance in the world without the slightest bit of prejudice."

In February spring training started up. Rickey, having learned a lesson from the year before, held training camp in Cuba, not Florida. Cuba didn't have the race problems that Florida did. On November 18 of the previous year, Rachel had given birth to Jackie Junior. Robinson was now a father and a proud one. He hated having to leave his little family for Cuba, but without enough money to bring Rachel and Jackie Junior with him, he had no choice.

Three other black players had joined the Royals—Roy Campanella, Don Newcombe, and Roy Partlow. When the Royals and Dodgers reached Cuba, Rickey had the black players stay in a dingy downtown hotel, while the rest of the Royals were quartered in the newly built National Military Academy. Robinson was angry about this and at first thought the Cuban government was to blame. Later he found out that Rickey had ordered the accommodations. He didn't want any racial incidents jeopardizing his great experiment. He wanted the training session to be "perfectly smooth." Robinson contained his anger and got to work.

Reporting to camp thirty pounds overweight, Robinson concentrated on getting into shape and playing ball. Then, just as he began to get in the swing of things, a new challenge was thrown at him. Rickey wanted him to play first base—a position he had never played before. Robinson felt more comfortable playing second base, his usual position, but he realized that if he was ever to become a Dodger, the only vacancy was at first base.

Robinson's first preseason game was against the Dodgers. Rickey had told him that if he wanted acceptance from the

Dodgers, he had to wow them with his play. And wow them he did. Besides two hits, he had thirteen putouts, or, in other words, for thirteen times he was the final player in a play that resulted in an out. His play was impressive, but the Dodgers didn't seem to notice. The team was ice-cold to him. One reporter concluded that the only thing keeping Robinson from becoming a Dodger was "the attitude of the players." Leo Durocher, the Dodgers' manager, however, did praise Robinson. He told a reporter, "He's my type of ballplayer. Jackie can hit, run, and field. What more can a manager ask of a player?"

❝Jackie Robinson is the loneliest man I have ever seen in sports.**❞**

—JIMMY CANNON,
SPORTSWRITER

Robinson sensed that the Dodgers were cold to him, but he didn't learn until much later just how much they didn't want him to play on their team. Before the games in Panama, a few players circulated a petition to keep Robinson off the Dodgers. While the players who started the petition were all southerners, not all southerners signed the petition. Pee Wee Reese from Kentucky, who later became a good friend of Robinson's, declared that Robinson "had a right to be there, too."

Word about the petition spread, and Rickey caught wind of it. His reaction was swift and brutal. First he turned the team's manager, Leo Durocher, loose on the men responsible. In the middle of the night Durocher hauled all the Dodgers out of their beds and let them have it. He told them that he didn't care what color a player was, if he was yellow or black or if he had stripes like a zebra. If he said the man could play, then he could play. Rickey then summoned the ringleaders of the petition to his hotel room. After telling them off, he offered to trade any player who didn't want to remain on the team. "No player on this club," he said, "will have anything to say about who plays or who does not play on it." Two Dodgers took him up on his offer.

It seemed that Robinson would never get his chance in the majors. Then, on April 9, 1947, something happened that moved events along very quickly. Leo Durocher was unexpectedly suspended from baseball for one year for conduct "detrimental to baseball." Durocher supposedly allowed gambling to take place in the Dodgers' clubhouse. Rickey was not only without a manager, he also had a scandal on his hands. He needed to take the focus away from the news about Durocher, and what better way than by making even bigger news? That same day, as the Royals and Dodgers played a preseason game in Ebbets Field, reporters in the press box were each handed a sheet of paper. The reporters silently read the following announcement: *The Brooklyn Dodgers today purchased the contract of Jackie Roosevelt Robinson from the Montreal Royals. He will report immediately.*

The next morning Robinson signed a contract with the Brooklyn Dodgers. His salary was the minimum for a player in the major leagues: $5,000 for the year. On April 15, 1947, Robinson put on his Dodger uniform, with the number 42 on the back, and made his debut in the major leagues. A large crowd had turned out for the season opener against the Boston Braves. Among the fans in the stands, Robinson knew, were Rachel and his infant son, Jackie Junior. Although the Dodgers won the game 5–3, Robinson didn't do much to help. He went hitless and, still learning to play first base, didn't field well. Later he said of that game, "I did a miserable job. There was an overflow crowd at Ebbets Field. If they expected any miracles out of Robinson, they were sadly disappointed."

JACKIE ROBINSON'S DEBUT AS A BROOKLYN DODGER

April 15, 1947, Ebbets Field

	Pos	AB	R	H	RBI
Jackie Robinson	1b	3	1	0	0

Used ticket stubs from Jackie Robinson's first game as a Brooklyn Dodger can sell today for as much as $2,000 each.

Robinson's game picked up, and after his first week of play he had scored five hits. The fans responded and attendance soared. Each time he stepped to the plate, he was cheered. Outside the clubhouse fans waited patiently, some with I'm for Jackie buttons pinned to their clothes. As soon as he came out, they mobbed him for autographs.

His biggest fans were black people and young people of all races. Many blacks who came to see Robinson play hadn't previously been baseball fans. In Robinson, though, they saw someone who was fighting an important battle for all of them. They responded by going to the ballparks in droves and cheering him on. Young fans also came to the stands. According to Robinson, "The very young seemed to have no hang-up at all about my being black. They just wanted me to be good, to deliver, to win." He especially remembered one early game in which a small white child "in the midst of a racially tense atmosphere . . . cried out, 'Attaboy, Jackie.' It broke the tension and it made me feel I had to succeed."

If the fans were welcoming, Robinson's fellow teammates were not. Because of Rickey, no player dared to confront Robinson, but most were cold and unfriendly. Robinson didn't let on how his teammates were treating him. To the press, he said that all the players worked well together. They were "a swell bunch." In reality, Robinson was a lonely man. One sportswriter, after visiting him in his hotel room, described the scene he found upon entering: "Jackie is sitting on his bed. The room is dark, the shades are halfway, and here is a lonely guy. His head is sunk in his hands. He feels friendless."

On April 22 the Dodgers played the Philadelphia Phillies for three games at Ebbets Field. The Phillies' manager, Ben Chapman, a southerner from Alabama, baited Robinson from the dugout and encouraged other players to do the same. They let loose with an unending stream of insults and abuse. Robinson was stunned. He hadn't expected this reaction in his own ballpark and from a northern team. He had trouble concentrating and didn't play well. Later he said, "This day, of all the unpleasant days in my life, brought me nearer to cracking up than I ever had been."

As he stood at the plate, listening to the abuse, he fantasized about throwing down his bat and striding over to the Phillies dugout, grabbing a player, and smashing his teeth with his fist. The image was tempting. Then he thought of Mr. Rickey.

"Mr. Rickey had come to a crossroads and made a lonely decision. I was at a crossroads. I would make mine. I would stay."

The Dodgers had two more games to play against Philly. The abuse continued. Then, in game three, something amazing happened. The other Dodger players had heard the abuse that was being heaped on their teammate. They saw the dignified way that Robinson reacted. Eddie Stanky, the Dodger second baseman, could finally stand it no longer. He faced the Phillies dugout and screamed, "Why don't you yell at somebody who can answer back?" The other Dodgers spoke out to the press, complaining of the treatment Robinson had received. The press went with the story, and soon Chapman found himself in hot water. When the Dodgers came to Philadelphia, Chapman was in danger of losing his job over the incident. Robinson agreed to pose with him to show that there were no hard feelings. Robinson later confessed, "Having my picture taken with this man was one of the most difficult things I had to make myself do."

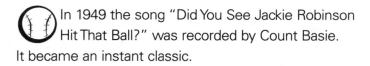 In 1949 the song "Did You See Jackie Robinson Hit That Ball?" was recorded by Count Basie. It became an instant classic.

Without a doubt, the games against the Phillies had been upsetting. However, something positive had come out of them. The Dodgers were now united. Branch Rickey put it best: "Chapman did more than anybody to unite the Dodgers. When he poured out that string of unconscionable abuse, he solidified and unified thirty men. . . . Chapman made Jackie a real member of the Dodgers."

Pee Wee Reese, the Dodgers' shortstop, also demonstrated to the world that Robinson belonged on the team. During one road game opposing players threw abuse at Robinson from the dugout. Getting no reaction from him, they then turned their attention to Reese, a Kentucky man. The players taunted Reese, asking how a southern man could play on the same team with a black man. Robinson, realizing that the hecklers were trying to get to him through Reese, felt each insult hit him "like a machine gun bullet." Pee Wee Reese responded by leaving his position and going over to stand next to Robinson. In a show of support, he placed a friendly hand on Robinson's shoulder. His action spoke volumes, telling fans and players alike that the Dodgers were united. The heckling stopped immediately, and a close and lasting friendship between the two men began that day.

It was a good thing Robinson had the support of Reese and his teammates. He needed it when early in the season he went into a slump. At one point, after twenty-one stands at the plate, he came away with only one hit. The Dodgers' new manager, Burt Shotton, wasn't concerned and made no attempt to bench Robinson. Robinson kept at it, and on May 1 the slump ended. Robinson hit a fastball into left field.

Right after Robinson came out of his slump, a plot was uncovered. The National League learned that the St. Louis Cardinal players were threatening to go on strike rather than play against Robinson. If this happened, other teams might also go on strike. Rickey and Robinson's great experiment would end before it ever had a chance to get off the ground. Ford C. Frick, the president of the National League, was informed about the impending strike. He wrote the following letter to the players, and its message, heard by all of baseball, rang loud and clear:

"If you do this you will be suspended from the league. You will find that the friends you think you have in the press box will not support you, that you will be outcasts. I do not care if half the league strikes. Those who do it will encounter quick retribution. All will be suspended and I don't care if it wrecks the National League for five years. This is the United States of America and one citizen has as much right to play as another. The National League will go down the line with Robinson what- ever the consequences. You will find if you go through with your intention that you have been guilty of complete madness."

Jackie Robinson won the very first Rookie of the Year award ever given.

The threat of a strike evaporated. Robinson's play continued to improve. By the end of the regular season he led the Dodgers in runs scored, bunt hits, and total bases. He was tied with teammate Pee Wee Reese for most home runs. And perhaps most impressively, he led the league with twenty-eight stolen bases.

September 23 was Jackie Robinson Day at Ebbets Field. Robinson was especially delighted to find his mother in the stands. Mallie had made her first airplane trip to be with her son on his special day. Robinson was given $10,000 worth of gifts—double his salary—including silverware, a television set, and a brand-new Cadillac. Three days later Robinson received another great honor. In a reception that the entire team attended, Robinson was presented with the very first Rookie of the Year award. Years later the award was named after Jackie Robinson.

The Dodgers went on to play the Yankees in the World Series. Robinson played well, batting .296 and error-free at first base, but the Dodgers ended up losing the series in the seventh game.

Robinson, now with a full year as a major leaguer under his belt, summed up his experience: "I had started the season as a lonely man. . . . I ended it feeling like a member of a solid team."

Chapter Nine

Champions at Last

Robinson's first year in the major leagues was a success. He was now one of the most famous men in the United States. A popularity poll placed him ahead of President Harry Truman and second only to singer Bing Crosby. Baseball had been good for Robinson, and Robinson had been good for baseball. Attendance at ballparks across the country had soared, and the reason was no secret. Fans were coming out to see Jackie Robinson play ball. "He became the biggest attraction in baseball since Babe Ruth," Red Barber, the Dodger radio announcer, declared.

In the spring of 1948 Robinson reported to training camp. He had spent the fall and winter traveling in the South and had eaten heartily. The pounds had piled on. Now, overweight and out of shape, he wasn't the same man who had left his teammates the past fall. Leo Durocher, back from his one-year suspension, was upset at Robinson's condition, and he made no bones about it. On first seeing Robinson, he ridiculed his weight gain in front of his teammates and the press. Robinson felt humiliated. Durocher then put Robinson through a series of grueling workouts. Slowly he began to shed his extra pounds.

By the time the season opened, Robinson had lost most of the weight. He was also back at second base, which he preferred to last season's first-base position. The season got off to a slow start for Robinson, and by June his batting average was only .270. Before long, though, his playing improved, and on June 24 he hit his first grand-slam homer. After a few more games his batting average jumped to .306. Robinson was back to his old form.

In September an incident occurred that Robinson called "the most important thing that happened to me in 1948." He was thrown out of a game for heckling the umpire. Baseball players are ejected all the time for heckling. Why was this such a big deal to Robinson? Because it made him feel like he was just like everyone else. As Robinson later explained: "He didn't pick on me because I was black. He was treating me exactly as he would any ballplayer who got on his nerves. That made me feel great." A newspaper headline summed up the incident: JACKIE JUST ANOTHER GUY.

Off the field, Robinson was proving to be "just another guy" as well. Like many husbands and fathers, he wanted a decent home for his wife and child. When they first moved to New York, he and Rachel had resided in a cramped hotel room in Manhattan. Rachel didn't even have a kitchen to cook their meals in and couldn't even heat up Jackie Junior's bottles. Then they moved to a seedy apartment in Brooklyn, where they were stuffed into a cramped back bedroom. Finally the Robinsons found a truly nice home, and in April they moved to Flatbush, renting the top floor of a two-family house. Some people weren't happy having a black family in their neighborhood, but other families welcomed them.

As the baseball season got under way, Rickey made a deal that sent Durocher to their rivals, the New York Giants. The Dodgers' new manager, Burt Shotton, was mild mannered and the complete opposite of Durocher. His low-key managing style, though, produced results. In early July the Dodgers had been in last place. By late August they had won seventeen of twenty-one games and had edged into first. In the race for the pennant, though, the Dodgers lost to the Braves.

By the season's end Robinson had the highest batting average of any Dodger and led his team in runs batted in. His

---

He could beat you in a lot of ways.

—YOGI BERRA

---

fielding was rated the best in the National League. Still, Robinson was unhappy with his performance. He knew he could have done better and vowed to improve in the next season.

With the start of the 1949 season, a new Jackie Robinson steamrolled into camp. Unlike the previous year, he was trim and eager to work. He practiced his sliding technique, and he spent hours hitting balls off a tee. "They'd better be rough on me this year," he told a reporter, "because I'm going to be rough on them." With three years in the Dodger organization, Robinson felt he had lived up to his bargain with Rickey. Baseball was slowly becoming integrated. Robinson now believed he was free to be himself.

For three long years Robinson had bottled up his feelings. He was expected to accept abuse but to say and do nothing. This would have been hard for any person, but for Robinson it had been doubly hard. By nature he was a man who hated injustice and longed to speak out against it. Now that the constraints were off, a new Robinson emerged. This Robinson spoke his mind freely with reporters. If he didn't like an umpire's call, he said so, and loudly. He argued with players and coaches on opposing teams.

Not everyone liked the new Robinson. The press, in particular, grew increasingly critical of him. Many preferred Roy Campanella, a popular black player on the Dodgers. Campanella's personality was the exact opposite of Robinson's. He was easy-going and liked to have a good time. Racial inequalities didn't seem to bother him. He often advised Robinson not to let discrimination upset him. After all, he reminded him, life in the majors sure was a lot more comfortable than life in the Negro Leagues. When Robinson complained of opposing players calling him names, Campanella claimed not to have heard the insults at all. Why couldn't Robinson be more like his teammate, the press wondered, and not rock the boat?

No matter what Robinson said or didn't say, it seemed that the press went out of its way to blame him. Once, when all the Dodgers complained about an unfair play, the press reported that only Robinson had done so. The league fined him. Another time a police officer claimed that Robinson had kicked a hole in a door after losing a game. Robinson's teammate, Preacher Roe, swore Robinson hadn't done it. (And Preacher Roe would have known. He had been the culprit.) Still, Robinson was again fined.

As usual, Robinson got off to a slow start when the 1949 season opened. After thirteen games he was hitting around .200. He seemed to have confidence, though, that he would rebound, and he did. By June his average had bounced up to .344, and by July it had soared to .361. By the end of the season he led the league in hitting, stolen bases, and double plays. The Dodgers won the pennant, faced the Yankees in the World

> **❝**He was the greatest competitor I've ever seen. I've seen him beat a team with his bat, his ball, his glove, his feet, and, in a game in Chicago one time, with his mouth.**❞**
>
> —DUKE SNIDER, TEAMMATE

Series, and lost—again. Despite the loss, Robinson was named the National League's MVP that November. It was, Robinson said, "the nicest thing that could have happened to me."

In January 1950 the Robinsons had a daughter, whom they named Sharon. The expanding family bought a house and moved from Brooklyn to St. Albans in Queens, New York. Robinson could afford the move because he had recently signed a new contract with the Dodgers, one for $35,000. He was now the highest-paid member on the team.

The Dodgers had high hopes for the 1950 season. Burt Shotton, the manager, was positive they would win the World Series. Robinson felt the same. Unfortunately, the Dodgers didn't even win the pennant, losing to the Phillies. Robinson had slowed down a bit and stole only twelve bases that year. (The previous year he'd stolen thirty-seven.) Still, his hitting remained strong. He finished the season with a .328 average. According to Dodgers coach Jake Pitler, he was still the "indispensable man. When he hits, we win. When he doesn't, we just don't look the same."

While much of the heckling and abuse that Robinson had faced was dying down, it had not gone away altogether. In May 1950, while in Cincinnati to play the Reds, Robinson learned a disturbing bit of news. The FBI informed him that a death threat against him had been sent to the Reds, the police, and a newspaper. The letter claimed that Robinson would be shot if he played that day at Crosley Field. When his teammates found out about the threat, one player half jokingly declared they should all wear Robinson's number 42 on their uniforms. That way the shooter wouldn't know which player to aim for. Robinson refused to be intimidated and played, to thunderous applause. The game went on without a hitch.

The end of the 1950 season brought about a big change for both Robinson and the Dodgers. Branch Rickey, the man Robinson trusted most in baseball, was leaving. A power struggle had occurred between Rickey and Walter O'Malley, a Dodger executive. Rickey ended up selling his share of the Dodgers to O'Malley, and O'Malley took over as president and general manager. O'Malley disliked Rickey so much that he told the Dodger players he would fine them one dollar each time he heard Rickey's name on their lips. Robinson remained loyal to his old friend and let it be known that he would always respect

Rickey and be grateful to him for giving him his chance in base-ball. This did not endear him to O'Malley, and the two men never became close.

When Robinson started the new season, he found the team had a new manager as well. Burt Shotton had been let go, and in his place was Charlie Dressen. Dressen, like Durocher, was as aggressive as Shotton had been mild and was eager to win the elusive World Series for the Dodgers. Robinson was in full agreement that the championship was long overdue, and he quickly fell in with the new manager's ways. Later he was to call Dressen his favorite manager.

JACKIE ROBINSON IN HOLLYWOOD

In 1950 Jackie Robinson flew to Hollywood to star in a movie called *The Jackie Robinson Story*. Robinson wasn't a professional actor, so the director, Alfred Green, told him to "just be yourself." Since the film was about baseball, Robinson had to perform baseball plays over and over for the camera. He told a reporter, "I never had any spring training in which I worked any harder." When the movie premiered on May 16, critics praised Robinson's natural acting ability, and the movie enjoyed modest success at the box office.

The Dodgers didn't make the World Series that year—they lost the National League pennant to the New York Giants. But Robinson had many outstanding games. One in particular showcased his competitiveness. On the last day of the regular season the Dodgers needed to beat the Phillies in order to face the Giants in the play-offs. In the eighth inning the Dodgers tied the game, and the score was 8–8. For three more innings the score remained unchanged. In the twelfth inning a Phillies player hit a ball to second base—right at Robinson. If Jackie didn't make the catch, the game would be over. It was now past six o'clock, dusk, and hard to see. The ball passed second base in a blur. According to a sportswriter who saw the play, Robinson "flings himself headlong at right angles to the flight of the ball, for an instant his body is suspended in midair, then somehow the outstretched glove intercepts the ball inches off the ground." It was an amazing catch by an amazing player. Two innings later Robinson hit a home run, winning the game.

The Dodgers by now had come close to winning the World Series many times. Dodger fans had a saying, "Wait till next year." Sometimes it must have felt that next year would never come. In 1952 and 1953 the Dodgers again faced the Yankees in the World Series. Both years they lost. The year 1954 was a particularly bad one for the Dodgers, giving them their worst season since 1947. Just as they had in 1951, they lost the pennant to the New York Giants.

As the years passed, Robinson was slowing down. His legs grew tired, and old injuries bothered him more and more. His hair had gone gray, and a permanent spare tire sat around his middle. At the start of the 1955 season he was thirty-five years old. Many newspaper writers wondered in their columns when he was going to retire. But Robinson was still a competitor. He wanted to win, and he wanted to win the World Series.

Spring training opened on March 1, 1955, and Robinson was there in his Dodger uniform, ready to play. He worked out hard and impressed Walter Alston, who had taken over as manager the year before. When the new season started, the Dodgers were impressive, winning twenty-one of their first twenty-five games. When Robinson made a smart move, preventing a double play from the opposing team, one newspaper stated ROBINSON CAN STILL DO IT ALL.

During the season Robinson spent a lot of time on the bench, nursing old injuries. The rest of the team was able to carry on without him and won the pennant. Once again the Dodgers had made the World Series, and once again their opponents were the dreaded New York Yankees. Although Robinson's statistics for the series are not impressive, he was still able to inspire his team. In the first game Robinson stole home for the eighteenth time in his career. In game three he performed some of his trademark baserunning, astounding the home crowd, which applauded wildly. AGING ROBINSON SETS DODGERS AFIRE ran a headline the next day.

The series went to seven games. Would history repeat itself? Would the Dodger fans have to call out yet again, "Wait till next year"? Jackie Robinson was on the bench during the last game, but he cheered his team on, and he was there when they finally won. The Dodgers had done it. They were champions at last!

Chapter Ten

Hall-of-Famer

Although he was a World Series winner, Robinson still faced discrimination. He had recently moved into a new house, but the fight to get it had been long and fierce. Soon after the Robinsons' third and last child, David, was born, Jackie and Rachel had decided that a bigger house was needed. Rachel was also tired of the fans who came around day and night, seeking autographs or wanting a glimpse of their favorite Dodger. Sometimes fans even came during dinner and didn't understand why Robinson couldn't come to the door.

Because she had more free time, Rachel took over the chore of house hunting. Both she and Jackie wanted a home outside of the city. Rachel looked at many houses, yet whenever she expressed interest in a particular place, the house was mysteriously withdrawn from the market or else its price shot up dramatically. This happened time and time again. A newspaper reporter heard about the trouble Rachel was having and wrote a story describing how racial prejudice was keeping the Robinsons from buying a home. Stamford, a city in Connecticut, was profiled in the article, although it certainly wasn't the only town that had shown discrimination. When the article appeared, many town leaders were embarrassed and decided to show the world that Stamford wasn't a prejudiced place. A group formed a committee and volunteered to help Rachel. While she didn't find a house, she did find five acres on which to build. In 1955 the Robinsons moved into their twelve-room dream home.

❝A life is not important except in the impact it has on other lives.❞

—JACKIE ROBINSON

The 1956 season would become Robinson's last in major league baseball. Still, when he reported to training camp that spring, he hadn't made up his mind when he would retire. No matter what his decision, he was determined to give the team the best he had. He focused his attention on winning that year's pennant and, hopefully, another World Series. Although he was often benched during the first few months, by August he was back in the lineup and contributing to his team. In his first game back, he scored a two-run homer, then won the game with a single. His inspired play continued through September, helping to clinch the pennant on the last day of the regular season.

Once again the Dodgers were in the World Series, and once again they were facing the Yankees. This time Robinson played in all seven games. His most important game was the sixth. Scoreless after nine innings, Robinson hit a line drive to left field in the tenth, allowing the Dodgers to win the game and tie up the series 3–3. Back in the dugout, Robinson received a hero's welcome. Robinson had kept the team's dreams of a repeat alive. Unfortunately, the Dodgers lost the next game and the series.

Robinson's last season as a Dodger was an improvement over the previous one. He played in more games, batted in more runs (ten of them homers), and scored more runs. He had proved that he could still be a valuable commodity for the Dodgers. Jackie figured he had at least one more season left in him. Still, there was no denying that he was older now. He gained weight easily and found it hard to take off, and he had numerous injuries. Most importantly, he missed Rachel and the children when he traveled with the team. He ended the 1956 season uncertain about the future.

Then fate stepped in to make the decision for him. That

December, Chock Full o' Nuts, a chain of coffee shops, offered Robinson an executive position as director of personnel. Robinson, who had always been interested in business, accepted the offer and decided to retire from baseball. A few years back he had signed an exclusive contract with *Look* magazine, agreeing to allow them to announce his retirement. In return he would receive $50,000. Usually when a player retired, he would inform the team and hold a press conference. Because of his agreement with *Look,* Robinson couldn't do this. He remained silent.

❝You opened the door for me and others who followed you and when you opened it you threw it wide open.❞
—BROOKS LAWRENCE, NEGRO LEAGUE PITCHER
WHO LATER PLAYED MAJOR LEAGUE BASEBALL

On December 12, the same day that he signed his contract with Chock Full o' Nuts, Robinson received a call from Buzzy Bavasi, the Dodgers' manager. Bavasi got straight to the point. He told Robinson that he had been traded to the Dodgers' rival team, the New York Giants. Robinson wanted to tell his manager that he was no longer Dodger property to be traded. Instead he bit his tongue, remembering the deal he had made with *Look.*

Robinson had no choice but to pretend to the Dodgers and the press that he would be joining the Giants. Then the

> **"**Every time I look at my pocketbook, I see Jackie Robinson.**"**
>
> —WILLIE MAYS

Look article came out. Many people in baseball were outraged. The Dodger management felt betrayed because Robinson hadn't told them he was retiring. Of course, *they* had never told *Robinson* he was going to be traded. Some members of the press were angry that Robinson had given *Look* the scoop. Others were more understanding and felt that it was Robinson's right to do as he chose. As for Robinson, he believed, "I was even with baseball and baseball with me. The game had done much for me, and I had done much for it."

The Giants still wanted Robinson. They offered him a much higher salary if he would agree to play. Robinson, although tempted, turned them down. On a cold day in January he returned to the Dodger clubhouse to clean out his locker for the last time. Robinson was leaving major league baseball the same way he had entered it—in a storm of controversy.

On a dark, gray day in July 1962, Jackie Roosevelt Robinson stood on a podium in Cooperstown, New York. He was forty-three years old, and his hair was completely white. He had been retired from baseball for five years. As Robinson gazed out at the crowds who had gathered to see him, he must have reflected on the long road that had led to this day, the day he would be inducted into the National Baseball Hall of Fame.

In order to qualify for induction, baseball's highest honor, a player must have been retired for five years, which Robinson was, and have made a great contribution to the game. By anyone's standards Robinson certainly had. The plaque that he received that day, which can be found in the Cooperstown Hall of Fame, states those qualifications:

LEADING N.L. BATTER IN 1949. HOLDS FIELDING MARK FOR SECOND BASEMAN PLAYING IN 150 OR MORE GAMES WITH .992. LED N.L. IN STOLEN BASES IN 1947 AND 1949. MOST VALUABLE PLAYER IN 1949. LIFETIME BATTING AVERAGE .311. JOINT RECORD HOLDER FOR MOST DOUBLE PLAYS BY SECOND BASEMAN, 137 IN 1951. LED SECOND BASEMEN IN DOUBLE PLAYS 1949–50–51–52.

Even with these amazing stats to his credit, Robinson hadn't thought it likely that he would get in, especially not on his first try. Players are voted into the Hall of Fame by sportswriters, and Jackie felt that he was too controversial a figure— that he had argued with too many sportswriters in his day. He once even made a bet with sportswriter Dick Young that he wouldn't be elected. In his first year of eligibility Robinson lost

What Jackie Robinson Started

Once Jackie Robinson broke baseball's color barrier, complete integration didn't happen overnight. It was a long, slow process. In 1951 fourteen blacks played in the majors. By 1953 only six of the sixteen major league teams had integrated. In 1955, ten years after Robinson first signed with the Dodgers, there were almost forty major league players who were black. The only teams without a black player were the Boston Red Sox, the Philadelphia Phillies, and the Detroit Tigers. It took until 1959 for all teams to be integrated. The Boston Red Sox were the last to do so.

that bet to Young. He was elected with 124 out of 160 ballots cast for him.

When he first heard the news, Robinson was uncharacteristically at a loss for words. Later he wrote about his feelings in a column for the *Amsterdam News.* "I just want to say that if this can happen to a guy whose parents were virtually slaves, a guy from a broken home, a guy whose mother worked as a domestic from sunup to sundown for a number of years; if this can happen to someone who, in his early years, was a delinquent, and who learned that he had to change his life—

then it can happen to you . . . out there who think that life is against you."

After the plaque was unveiled, Robinson made his acceptance speech. Then he called three people to join him at the podium—his wife, Rachel, his mother, Mallie, and a man who had been like a father to him, Branch Rickey. He told the audience that having these three people with him on this day made "the honor complete." "And I don't think," he continued, "I will ever come down from Cloud Nine."

Snapping the Barbed Wire of Prejudice

A fter retiring from baseball, Robinson continued to speak out against social injustice. He led a fund-raising campaign for the National Association for the Advancement of Colored People (NAACP), giving speeches all across the country. His efforts helped raise over $1 million in contributions. Later Robinson became involved in politics, campaigning first for Richard Nixon for president and later for Nelson Rockefeller for governor of New York. (Both men lost the elections.) For a time Robinson also had a weekly radio program, and he wrote columns for the *Amsterdam News* and the *New York Post*, expressing his views on sports as well as on topics of the day. In 1964 Robinson helped establish the Freedom National Bank, a black-owned financial institution in Harlem, New York. The bank loaned money to black businesspeople when many white-owned banks wouldn't.

In December 1965 Robinson received bad news: Branch Rickey, his old friend and mentor, had died. Robinson felt the loss deeply. Three years later Robinson lost his mother, Mallie. His hardest loss, however, was when his oldest child, Jackie Junior, died in a car accident in 1971. Jackie Junior was only twenty-four at his death. Robinson was heartbroken, most especially because he had only recently reconnected with his son. Jackie Junior had fought in the Vietnam War and returned addicted to drugs. In 1968 he was arrested for possession. When Robinson heard the news, he wanted to disown his son. Later, though, after talking with him, he and Rachel decided to support Jackie Junior. He was admitted into a rehabilitation program and successfully beat his addiction. He then became a counselor, helping other young people to quit drugs. At his son's funeral Robinson took comfort at seeing the number of ex-addicts who attended. He knew that Jackie Junior had helped these people and that his life had not been wasted.

As he approached his fifties, Robinson's health grew worse. Shortly after he left baseball he had been diagnosed with diabetes, a disease in which the body doesn't process insulin efficiently. Robinson had learned how to give himself insulin shots, but as the years passed, he suffered many complications

Good-bye to Ebbets Field

On September 24, 1957, the Brooklyn Dodgers played their last game at Ebbets Field, their home ballpark. The team's owner, Walter O'Malley, had decided to move his team to sunny California. The Giants, another New York team, also left for California, leaving the Yankees as the city's only major league team until 1962, when the Mets came to Shea Stadium. In 1960 Ebbets Field was demolished. An apartment complex named after Jackie Robinson now stands on the site.

of the disease. His eyesight began to fail, and he found it increasingly difficult to walk. In 1968 he suffered a mild heart attack. Still, Robinson didn't let illness slow him down, and he continued to work and speak out.

In June 1972 Jackie Robinson attended a ceremony at the new Dodger Stadium in Los Angeles. The ceremony commemorated the twenty-fifth anniversary of Robinson's first major league season. Nearly blind, he wasn't able to catch a ball a fan threw and the ball hit his head, knocking off his Dodgers' cap. Still, he proudly, if stiffly, walked across the ballpark diamond when the Dodger organization retired his number. Later he called the experience "one of the greatest moments of my life."

Much had changed in baseball in the twenty-five years since Robinson first put on a Dodger uniform. Baseball was now completely integrated. African Americans played for all major league teams, and no one thought twice about it. Although these new players didn't suffer the abuse Robinson took, many were aware of the debt they owed Robinson. Hank Aaron, the man who broke Babe Ruth's lifetime home run record, once said, "I realize the only reason I made it was because of a man like Jackie Robinson. I would like the next generation to understand a man who stood so tall." But Robinson's legacy went beyond baseball. Many black athletes in other sports, such as Bill Russell, Kareem Abdul-Jabbar, and Arthur Ashe, have credited him with inspiring them.

A few short months after his number was retired, on October 24, Jackie Robinson died of a heart attack. He was fifty-three. At his funeral Jesse Jackson, an important leader in the civil rights movement, gave the eulogy. He said that Robinson had "snapped the barbed wire of prejudice. . . . In his last dash, Jackie stole home and Jackie is safe."

Many years later, on April 15, 1997, Jackie Robinson became the only player in major league baseball whose number was retired by every team. It was baseball's way of saying there would never be another player like him. And there never will be.

PERSONAL STATISTICS

Name:
Jack Roosevelt Robinson

Nickname:
Jackie

Born:
January 31, 1919

Died:
October 24, 1972

Height:
5'11"

Weight:
195 lbs.

Batted:
Right

Threw:
Right

BATTING STATISTICS

Year	Team	Avg	G	AB	Runs	Hits	2B	3B	HR	RBI	SB
1947	BD	.297	151	590	125	175	31	5	12	48	29
1948	BD	.296	147	574	108	170	38	8	12	85	22
1949	BD	.342	156	593	122	203	38	12	16	124	37
1950	BD	.328	144	518	99	170	39	4	14	81	12
1951	BD	.338	153	548	106	185	33	7	19	88	25
1952	BD	.308	149	510	104	157	17	3	19	75	24
1953	BD	.329	136	484	109	159	34	7	12	95	17
1954	BD	.311	124	386	62	120	22	4	15	59	7
1955	BD	.256	105	317	51	81	6	2	8	36	12
1956	BD	.275	117	357	61	98	15	2	10	43	12
	Totals	.308	1382	4877	947	1518	273	54	137	734	197

FIELDING STATISTICS

Year	Team	Pos.	G	C	PO	A	E	DP	FLD%
1947	BD	1B	151	1,431	1,323	92	16	144	.989
1948	BD	2B	116	16	308	315	13	80	.980
		1B	30	219	203	15	1	16	.995
		3B	6	636	3	12	1	1	.937
1949	BD	2B	156	832	395	421	16	119	.981
1950	BD	2B	144	760	359	390	11	133	.986
1951	BD	2B	150	832	390	435	7	137	.992
1952	BD	2B	146	773	353	400	20	113	.974
1953	BD	OF	76	5	145	9	3	0	.974
		3B	44	46	34	84	3	14	.975
		2B	9	41	16	25	0	7	1.000
		1B	6	121	41	5	0	4	1.000
		SS	1	157	2	3	0	0	1.000
1954	BD	OF	74	23	110	4	0	0	1.000
		3B	50	145	43	95	7	6	.952
		2B	4	114	13	10	0	0	1.000
1955	BD	3B	84	6	74	180	9	18	.966
		OF	10	12	11	1	0	0	1.000
		1B	1	12	11	0	1	0	.917
		2B	1	263	4	2	0	1	1.000
1956	BD	3B	72	2	61	173	8	15	.967
		2B	22	75	39	49	1	17	.989
		1B	9	89	67	8	0	5	1.000
		OF	2	242	2	0	0	0	1.000
	Total		1,364	6,852	4,007	2,728	117	830	.983

BIBLIOGRAPHY

Brashler, William. *The Story of Negro League Baseball.* New York: Ticknor & Fields, 1994.

Coombs, Karen Mueller. *Jackie Robinson: Baseball's Civil Rights Legend.* New Jersey: Enslow Publishers, Inc., 1997.

Dingle, Derek T. *First in the Field: Baseball Hero Jackie Robinson.* New York: Hyperion, 1998.

Falkner, David. *Great Time Coming: The Life of Jackie Robinson, from Baseball to Birmingham.* New York: Simon & Schuster, 1995.

Rampersad, Arnold. *Jackie Robinson: A Biography.* New York: Alfred A. Knopf, 1997.

Robinson, Jackie. *I Never Had It Made.* New Jersey: Ecco Press, 1995.

WEB SITES

Baseball Almanac—Jackie Robinson

http://www.baseball-almanac.com/players/p_robij0.shtml

Quotes by and about Jackie Robinson abound on this site. You'll also find extensive statistics, speeches, and even a poem or two.

The Jackie Robinson Society

http://www.utexas.edu/students/jackie

This student-based site from the University of Texas features articles about Jackie Robinson as well as a photo gallery.

Negro League Baseball Players Association

http://www.nlbpa.com

Learn all about the athletes and teams that made up the Negro Leagues.

TIME 100: Heroes & Icons—Jackie Robinson

http://www.time.com/time/time100/heroes/profile/robinson01.html

Read Hank Aaron's moving tribute to Jackie Robinson.

INDEX

A

Aaron, Hank, 96
Abdul-Jabbar, Kareem, 96
Alston, Walter, 82
Amsterdam News, 90, 93
Anderson, Carl, 16, 17
Ashe, Arthur, 96
Atascadero, California, 29

B

Baltimore, Maryland, 56
Barber, Red, 73
Bartlett, Ray, 14, 26
Basie, Count, 68
Bates, Colonel Paul, 34, 35
Bavasi, Buzzy, 88
Bears, Honolulu, 29
Bell, Cool Papa, 40, 41
Berra, Yogi, 75
Betzel, Bruno, 58
Braves, Boston, 65, 75
Brooklyn, New York, 45,
    46, 47, 49, 50, 75, 78
Bulldogs, Pasadena Junior
    College, 19, 20, 22

C

Cairo, Georgia, 5, 7, 9
Campanella, Roy, 62, 76–77
Campanis, Al, 55
Camp Breckinridge,
    Kentucky, 35, 36
Camp Wheeler, Georgia,
    35
Cannon, Jimmy, 63
Cardinals, St. Louis, 70
Chapman, Ben, 67, 68, 69
Chicago, Illinois, 41, 78
Chock Full o' Nuts, 88
Colonels, Louisville, 58, 59
Cooperstown, New York,
    89
Crawfords, Pittsburgh, 38
Cronin, Joe, 39–40
Crosby, Bing, 73
Crosley Field, 79
Crutchfield, Jimmie, 38, 39
Cuba, 61, 62

D

Daytona Beach, Florida,
    51–52, 54
Dodgers, Brooklyn, 33, 42,
    45, 55, 61, 62, 63, 64,
    65, 66, 67, 68, 69, 70,
    71, 75, 76, 77, 78, 79,
    80, 81, 82, 83, 85, 87,
    88, 89, 91, 95
Dodger Stadium, 95
Downs, Karl, 16
Dressen, Charlie, 80
Duffy, Hugh, 43
Durocher, Leo, 63, 64, 73,
    74, 75, 80
Dykes, Jimmy, 26

E

East-West All-Star game,
    41
Ebbets Field, 64, 65, 67, 71,
    95

F

FBI, 79
Fenway Park, Boston, 39
Flatbush, New York, 75
Fort Hood, Texas, 33
Fort Riley, Kansas, 31, 32
Foster, Andrew, 37
Freedom National Bank, 93
Frick, Ford C., 70

G

Giants, Jersey City, 1, 2, 3,
    56, 58
Giants, New York, 75, 81,
    82, 88, 89, 95
Glendale, California, 22
Glendale Junior College, 22
Green, Alfred, 80

H

Harlem, New York, 93
Heard, Sid, 13
Honolulu, Hawaii, 29
Hopper, Clay, 53, 54, 56, 60
Houston, Texas, 39

I

International League, 1

J

Jackie Robinson Day, 71
Jackie Robinson Story, The,
    80
Jackson, Jesse, 96
Jackson, "Shoeless" Joe, 7
Jersey City, New Jersey, 1, 2
John Muir Technical High
    School, 17, 18

L

Lawrence, Brooks, 88
Little World Series, 58, 59
Look magazine, 88, 89
Los Angeles, California, 95
Louis, Joe, 16, 31, 34
Louisville, Kentucky, 58, 59

M

Mays, Willie, 89
McGriff, Edna Sims, 9
McGriff, Washington, 9
Mets, New York, 95
Monarchs, Kansas City, 36,
    37, 38, 39, 40, 41, 42,
    45, 50
Montreal, Canada, 57, 59

N

National Association for
    the Advancement of
    Colored People
    (NAACP), 93
National Baseball Hall of
    Fame, 90
National League, 70, 76,
    78, 81
Negro Leagues, 36, 37, 38,
    39, 40, 41, 43–44, 50,
    77, 88
Newcombe, Don, 62
New Orleans, Louisiana, 51
New York Daily News, 50
New York Post, 93
Nixon, Richard, 93

O

Olympics, 17
O'Malley, Walter, 79, 80, 95
Orioles, Baltimore, 56
Otis, Phil, 3
Owens, Jesse, 17

P

Pacific Coast Negro Tennis Tournament, 18
Paige, Satchel, 41, 48
Panama, 63
Partlow, Roy, 62
Pasadena, California, 1, 7, 17
Pasadena Junior College, 19, 20, 21, 23, 24, 25, 53
Pasadena Star-News, 18
Pensacola, Florida, 51
Philadelphia, Pennsylvania, 68
Phillies, Philadelphia, 67, 68, 69, 78, 80, 91
Phoenix, Arizona, 21
Pitler, Jake, 78
Powers, Jimmy, 50

R

Rams, Los Angeles, 59
Reds, Cincinnati, 7, 79
Red Sox, Boston, 39, 40, 91
Reese, Pee Wee, 63, 69, 71
Reiser, Pete, 32
Rickey, Wesley Branch, 42, 43, 45, 46, 47, 48, 49, 50, 51, 53, 54, 56, 61, 62, 64, 67, 68, 69, 70, 75, 76, 79, 80, 92, 94
Robinson, David, 85
Robinson, Edgar, 10

Robinson, Frank, 23–24
Robinson, Jackie Junior, 62, 65, 75, 94
Robinson, Jack Roosevelt
army career, 30–35
birth, 5
as Brooklyn Dodger, 65–89
childhood, 5–18
college career, 19–27
as Montreal Royal, 1–3, 50–65
Negro Leagues career, 36–50
Robinson, Jerry, 5
Robinson, Mack, 17, 20, 22
Robinson, Mallie, 5, 6, 7, 8, 9, 11, 15, 26, 50, 71, 92, 94
Robinson, Rachel Isum, 25, 26, 30, 35, 36, 40, 46, 50, 51, 52, 55, 57, 61, 62, 65, 75, 85, 86, 87, 92, 94
Robinson, Ray, 34
Robinson, Sharon, 78
Robinson, Willa Mae, 8, 10
Rochelli, Lou, 55
Rockefeller, Nelson, 93
Roe, Preacher, 77
Rookie of the Year award, 71
Roosevelt Stadium, 1
Royals, Montreal, 1, 2, 3, 47, 49, 50, 51, 52, 53, 55, 56, 57, 58, 59, 61, 62, 64, 65
Russell, Bill, 96
Ruth, Babe, 73, 96

S

Sacramento, California, 21
Samuelson, Rube, 21

Sanford, Florida, 2, 52, 54, 56
Shea Stadium, 95
Shotton, Burt, 70, 75, 78, 80
Snider, Duke, 78
Southern California Junior Track Championships, 21
St. Albans, New York, 78
Stamford, Connecticut, 86
Stanky, Eddie, 68
Stearnes, Norman "Turkey," 41
Sukeforth, Clyde, 45, 46, 47
Syracuse, New York, 57

T

Thomas, Charles, 42, 43
Tigers, Detroit, 91
Truman, Harry, 73

U

University of California at Los Angeles (UCLA), 23, 24, 25, 26, 27, 53
University of Missouri, 33

W

Washington, Kenny, 59
White Sox, Chicago, 7, 26
Wilkinson, J. L., 40
World Series, 7, 71, 77–78, 80, 81, 82–83, 85, 86, 87
World War II, 30, 42

Y

Yankees, New York, 41, 71, 77, 81, 82, 87, 95
Young, Dick, 90, 91